WE

FOR

BEGINNERS

A Step By Step Guide On How To Weave, With Tips And Tricks, And With The Aid Of Pictures. Learn As A Beginner Everything You Need To Know In The World Of Weaving

By

Kathleen R. Barone.

Copyright © 2021 Kathleen R. Barone.

No warranties of any kind are implied. The contents of this book are derived from various sources. Please consult a licensed professional before attempting any techniques All rights reserved. No part of this book shall be reproduced, stored in a retrieval system, or transmitted by any means, electronic, mechanical, photocopying, recording, or otherwise, without written permission from the publisher. Although every precaution has been taken in the preparation of this book, the publisher and author assume no responsibility for errors or omissions. Nor is any liability assumed for damages resulting from the use of the information contained herein.

LEGAL NOTICE:

This book is copyright protected and is only for personal use. This book should not be amended or distributed, sold, quote, or paraphrased without the consent of the author or publisher.

DISCLAIMER:

The information contained in this book is for educational purposes only. All efforts have been executed to present accurate, reliable, and up-to-date information contained herein. By reading this document, the reader agrees that under no circumstances is the author responsible for any losses, direct or indirect, which are incurred as a result of the information contained in this book including errors, omissions, and inaccuracy

Table of Contents

INTRODUCTION 1
    WEAVING PROCESS 3
    TYPES OF WOVEN FABRICS 3
    ESSENTIAL ASSETS 5
CHAPTER ONE 20
TYPES OF LOOMS 20
    WEAVING AND LOOM BASICS 21
    TYPES OF LOOMS 22
    WHAT TO CONSIDER WHEN BUYING A LOOM 28
CHAPTER TWO 30
WEAVING TERMS 30
    YARN FIBERS 33
    YARN WEIGHT 36
    THE STANDARD YARN WEIGHT SYSTEM 37
CHAPTER THREE 39
HOW TO CHOOSE COORDINATIVE YARN COLORS .. 39
    SELECTION OF WARP YARN 52
    WARP YARN FOR TAPESTRY AND RUG WEAVING 53
    WARP YARNS FOR TOWELS, PLACEMATS, OR HOME TEXTILES 54
    WARP YARN FOR SCARVES, SHAWLS, OR APPAREL WEAVING 55

- WARP YARN FOR A RIGID HEDDLE LOOM 56
- THE SNAP TEST 56
- AN EXCEPTION TO THE SNAP TEST RULE 57
- YARNS RECOMMENDED FOR WARP AND WEFT.. 58

CHAPTER FOUR 61
WARP THE LOOM 61
- HOW TO WARP DIFFERENT LAP LOOMS 62
- TABBY WEAVE 65
- RYA KNOT 66
- STEPS TO CREATE RYA KNOTS 68

CHAPTER FIVE 71
WEAVING SHAPES 71
- HOW TO WEAVE A CIRCLE 72
- HOW TO WEAVE A RECTANGLE 74
- HOW TO WEAVE A TRIANGLE 74
- CREATE BLOCKS USING A STRAIGHT SLIT 75

CHAPTER SIX 84
SOUMAK WEAVING 84
- BASIC STEPS 85
- PILE WEAVE LOOPS 91

CHAPTER SEVEN 99
FINISH YOUR WOVEN PIECE 99
- MAKE YOUR LOOM 104

BRANCH WEAVING 110
SUMMER BRACELET 114

INTRODUCTION

Weaving, the process of forming a fabric by weaving two or more yarns or other materials at right angles. One of the most ancient basic arts for which archaeological evidence has been pointed out. The discoveries in the Czech Republic in the early 1990s indicate the possible origin of the Paleolithic some 27,000 years ago.

In addition, the first literature often mentions loom products. In primitive cultures, weaving was practiced primarily by women.

Although weaving developed independently in different parts of the world and was known in early Europe, its high development there in the Middle Ages was created by Eastern influences through the channels of Muslim culture. Byzantium became the center of silk weaving in the 6th century. Greece, Italy, and Spain became adept in the ninth century. In Flanders, the 10th century gained a high level of skill, especially in wool weaving. The Flemish weaving that was brought to England by the William Conquest and then Queen Elizabeth I gave a big boost to the handicrafts there, and Lancashire became an important center. Upholstery weaving was brought to high art in France. In colonial America, weaving was a household industry associated with agriculture.

Weaving and spinning inventions in the 18th century marked a transition from the ancient era of domestic handicrafts to today's vast and organized industry. The factory weaving machine system produces a standardized amount of material for mass consumption; the result is a loss of the distinctive elements of quality and design. The finest silk, velvet, tablecloths, and rugs were still woven on handicrafts.

WEAVING PROCESS

Stretching the warp strands, or longitudinal yarns, which should be very strong, is the first step in weaving. The weft, lint, or filler crosses the chain and connects the warp threads on both sides to create the wind. After chain tension, the three basic steps are: pulling or lifting any alternative warp thread or set of yarns to receive weft; take or insert weft; and press the slat or weft into the house to make the fabric solid. In most of the primitive weave, these operations were done by hand alone, for example, to make mats and attack bags. Gradually frames were used to stretch the chain evenly, and weft-throwing devices were used.

TYPES OF WOVEN FABRICS

Woven fabrics are classified according to texture or structure based on how warp and weft meet. The three basic weaves, of which others are variations, are plain, twill and satin. In plain weave, also known as chalice, tabby, taffeta, or home-woven weave, the weft passes through alternating warp threads, requiring only two straps. The relatively simple construction is suitable for cheap fabrics, heavy yarns, and printed patterns. Weaving baskets and monk's shawls, for example, or alternating fine and coarse yarns to generate ribbed and corded textiles like Bedford cord in the warp, picket and blur, and weft-ribbed poplin, rep, and grosgrain, are examples of variations.

The second primary weave, the heel, shows a diagonal pattern created by weft threads connecting two or four warp threads, moving one step to the right or left in each pick, and can be varied, such as spinal cord and corkscrew models. Due to their solid and tight texture, the corner fabrics are remarkable: gabardine, army, drill, and jeans. The satin weave has warp yarns that float or jump over the light-reflecting surface, giving a characteristic light. When the unbreaded fibers are in the weft, the texture is called satin.

Yarns are cut or uncut when they pass through additional wires that generate lines in fur textiles. Curved fabrics include terry and plush; piles of weft, velvet, and cord. In double weaving, two fabrics are woven simultaneously, each with warp and weft yarns, and joined together by joining individual yarns or adding the fifth set. Clothing can be made for extra warmth or strength to allow the use of cheap backing, or result in a different design or texture on each surface, such as steam mats, heavy upholstery, and machine straps. . Velvet is usually woven as a double fabric. In the case of rotary weaving, additional transfers made of filling yarns in circular motions are made of simple ornaments such as Swiss muslin dots. Pattern weaves are made by dividing the chain and weft into different groups. Simple geometric patterns can be woven on looms to operate the straps using a cam or drum holder.

For large curves and shapes, each shield must be adjusted separately. The jacquard loom attachment allows the machine weaving of the most complex patterns.

ESSENTIAL ASSETS

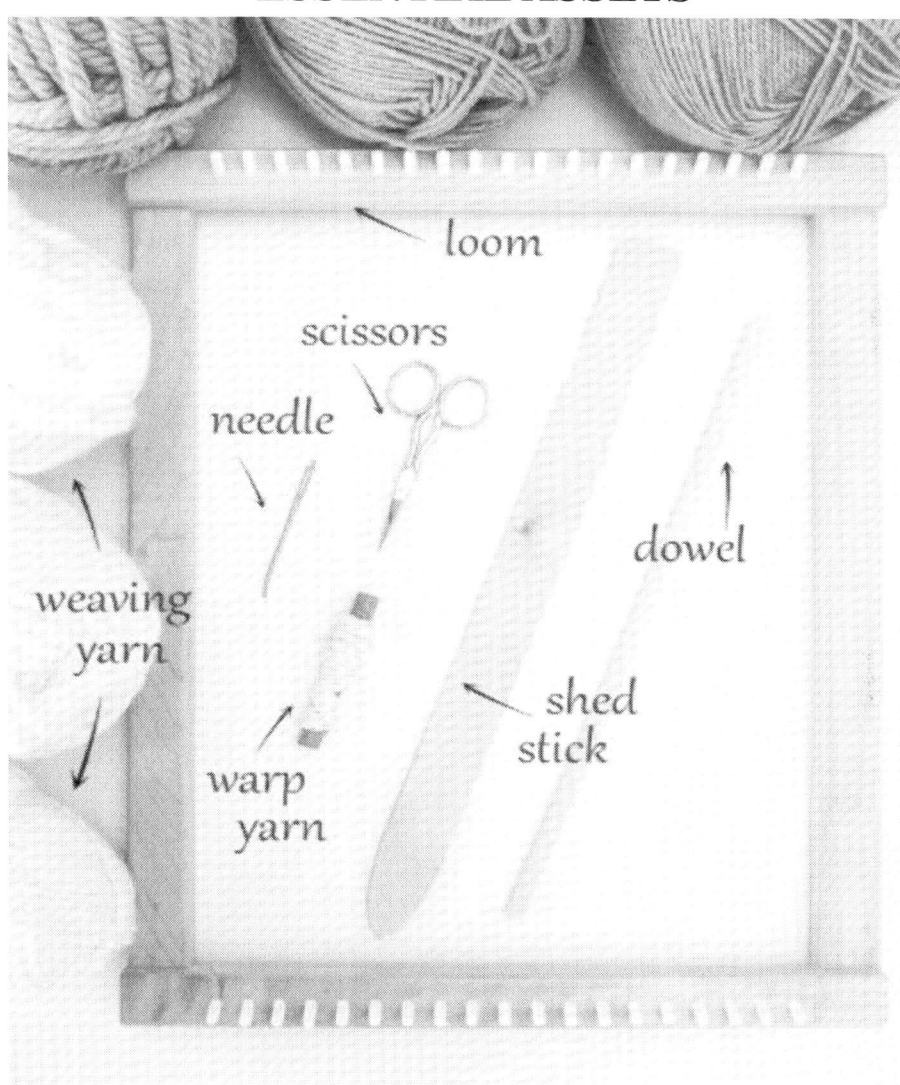

So, you just started weaving (or for a while) and you loved it! But he went beyond where to buy the most basic tools and supplies for weaving. When you do a google search, you come across all kinds of weaving sites: rigid hedge weaving, square weaving, stick weaving, and everything in between. You've recently found that the world of weaving is considerably larger than you previously imagined!

I know exactly how you feel. This was my experience when I first started weaving.

This was partly because there was no one I could ask about weaving. I didn't know any textures None of them. Oh, I've mixed a stick with a dozen knitters, crocheters, and a few more that can embroider (including me), but how do I find a texture? Well, it was like looking for a needle in a very large bundle of super huge yarns

But now, with some time and experience under my belt, I've finally figured out how to organize my tools and materials, as well as where to find them.

If you're looking for basics for weaving with your wheels - or have been weaving for some time and want to expand your repertoire of tools and materials - Let me share some of my favorite low-cost weaving supplies with you, along with where you can find them.

Tips & Warnings: Using the right search terms in any search for weaving tools and materials make a big difference. In the list below, I used the terms that gave me the best results.

1. **FRAMEWORK LOOM**

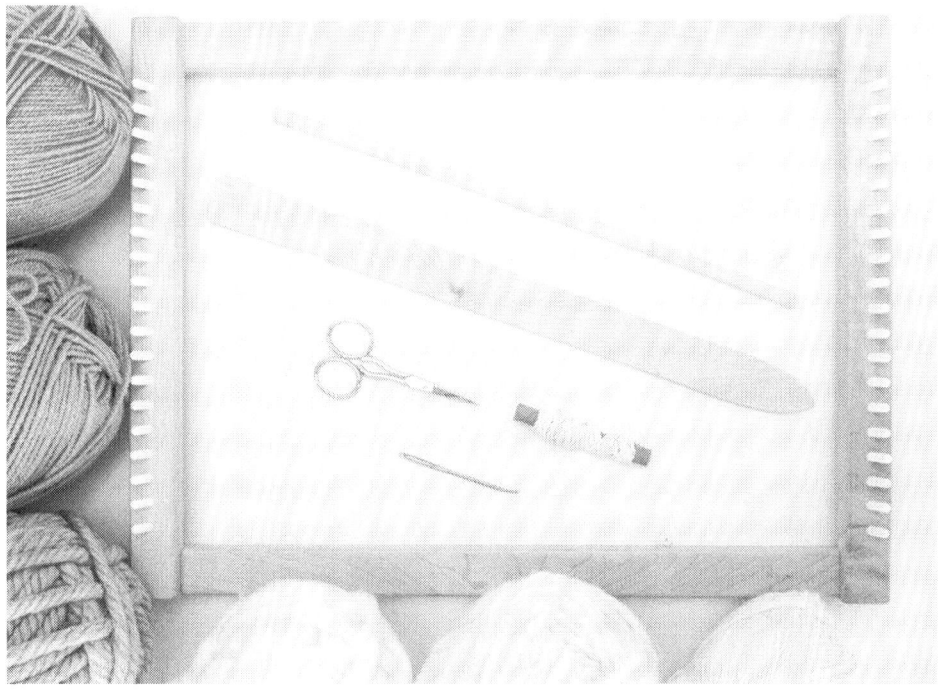

The type of loom I use for my wall weaves is called Frame Loom. This is because it is rectangular, just like a photo frame. There are two types of frames I use:

> Lap Loom

The first one is called Lap Loom. This type of framed loom is small, about 14 inches wide (with 12 inches of actual usable weaving space).

Start your search with these cost-effective weaving sheets, in two different sizes and prices: 14.5 ″ looms (budget-friendly version) and 14 ″ looms (handmade).

> Steep looms

Standing looms are sometimes described as scaffolding and are slightly larger than suits and have "arms". They allow the loom to be supported on the table by stretching the arms back to support the loom. After that, you can relax at a table and weave.

Note: During the online search, you can view three different versions of the frame texts. One is called Peg Loom. This type has an angle at the bottom and top of the loom. The second variation is called Newched Loom. This type has notches on the top and bottom of the loom. The third variation is called Tabbed Loom. This type has "ears" protruding from the top and bottom of the loom. Check out these helpful videos on twisting these types of framed looms:

2. TAPESTRY NEEDLE

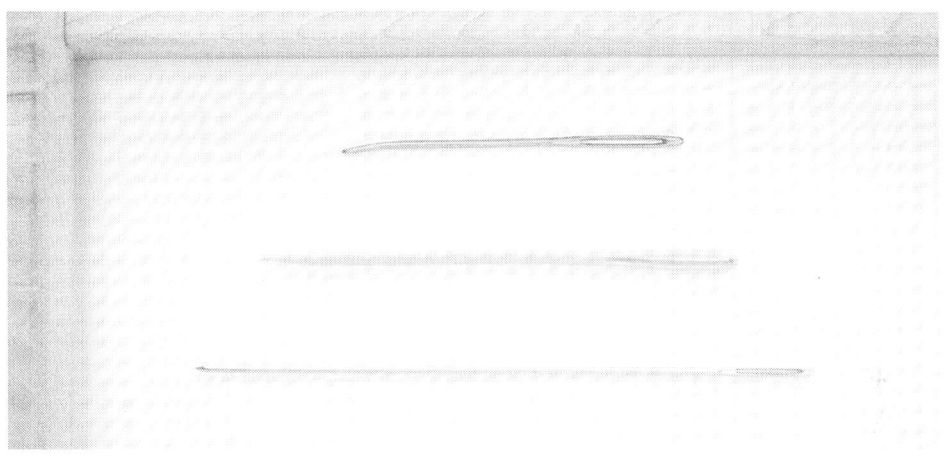

Tapestry needles come in a variety of shapes and sizes as well (as you can see from my collection above). You only need a basic weaving tool like this to get started, but it is always helpful to have at least 2 or 3 types when you are in the art of thread weaving.

> ### Straight and small weaving needle

When I first started weaving, I used a small 3-inch plastic needle that had large eyes and a flat tip (perfect for children, and yet I use it). The large needle eye allows me to use a wide range of threads of different "weights" or thicknesses.

For a cheap and easy-to-start plastic weaving needle, try this cheap option at The Unusual Pear on Etsy.

- **Curved weaving needle**

Once you get used to weaving, you need to buy a curved loom - this is a must in the weaving tool arsenal. Having my first needle with a curved tip was an absolute change in the game! This made my weaving time easier and a little faster. The advantage of having a curved tapestry needle at its edge is that it is much easier to get under its warp threads.

I use this curved loom and I love it!

- **Long weaving needle**

One of my most recent purchases was this long weaving needle. It is 5 inches long and, like a curved needle, speeds up the weaving process by passing through the warp thread much faster. I can't say enough about it - it's one of my favorite weaving tools!

3. WARP YARN

Cotton yarn

You can use almost any yarn to create a warp yarn - indeed. But perhaps the one that uses the weave the most for anything else is cotton - and for good reason. Cotton is soft and flexible, but sturdy and strong. This combination makes the perfect thread to create the chain.

White or cream - the basics

Each weaver must have at least one white or cream cotton thread in his arsenal. I recommend trying Lily Sugar n 'Cream's white and cream yarn. I have both.

Other colors

If you already have white or cream cotton yarn, you will probably want to experiment with color. There is something very interesting about the use of contrasting colors in warp yarns.

Other varieties

Overall, I got good results using other yarns to create warp yarns, including cheap acyl, hemp, and bamboo dyes - some of which I shared in this blog (I used acrylic yarn for these DIY woven pads and hemp yarn for this DIY pillow). All of these products, as well as HobbyCraft, Hobby Lobby, Michaels, and CraftOnline products, can be found at any local craft store or online store.

4. SHED STICK

A cast stick can be useful in some important ways.

First, it can be woven into the chain, rotated sideways, so that space can be moved or the thread can be pulled up over the chain without a needle.

Second, before you start to forget, a shed can be woven into the bottom. The casting rod provides a good base on which you can press your weaving stitches to keep the weaving beautiful and straight.

A variety of sizes and materials can be used to make the basic shed rods on Etsy.

When choosing the proper length, look for one that is broader than its warp wall to ensure even support from beginning to end.

You can also improvise by weaving wider weaves with a long piece of cardboard and narrower weaves with a ruler (as you did here).

5. WEAVING COMB

I still didn't have to buy a suitable texture for the simple reason that I didn't need it. I used a kitchen fork for all my weaving - and I mean EVERYTHING. This includes simple weaves like my DIY underlay for this very intricate wavy weave.

You can use something as cheap as a hair sorter (like this) or even a plastic brush. This is true! I've seen video tutorials where the textures used both.

But, if you, like me, want to get a proper comb for weaving at some point, let me refer to those who made my shortlist:

- ➢ 6-inch weaving comb
- ➢ 12-inch weaving comb
- ➢ Small weaving comb (for those small weaves)
- ➢ With a 10-tooth comb handle

6. SCISSORS

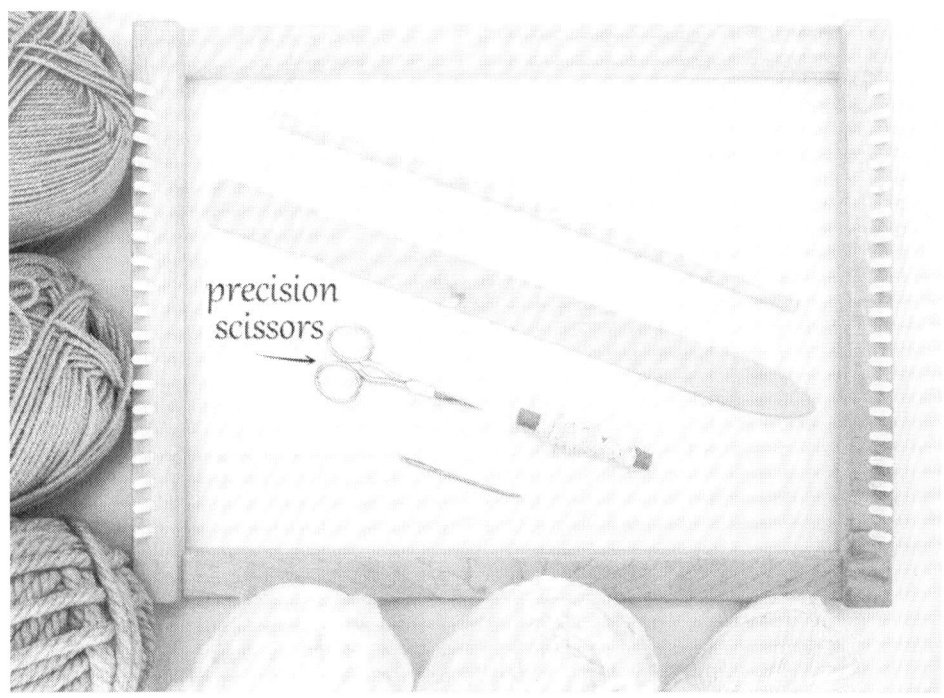

When I weave, I use two different types of scissors. Depending on the size and type of weaving, I frequently use the other, and occasionally both.

> ➢ Regular kitchen or craft scissors

Standard kitchen or craft scissors are perfect. They are nice to have on hand, for example, when cutting thick peeled yarns but can be used for any of their yarns. In my tutorials, you can often see me using our kitchen scissors. They are very suitable for most weaving projects.

➢ Precision scissors

I like to use smaller, precision scissors when working on weaving a smaller or finer yarn. This makes it easier to get into tight spaces if needed. Basic embroidery scissors, such as this pair, are what I use.

But there are many styles and colors to choose from, such as this cute freshman design or this stylish pair of black bonsai.

7. WEAVING YARNS

The good news is that the wall is available everywhere! And you can use almost any type, including acrylic (good for beginners as a cheap thread). Later, you may want to use wool or wool blends that are more durable. I've used a wide variety of brands, including Red Heart, Lion Brand, Wool-Ease (another Lion brand), Patons, and Bernat.

If you are a beginner, you may want to buy small packs of different colors like this or that. Great options, easy to budget.

Special and artistic yarns

You may find all kinds of speciality and artistic yarns online in a variety of sites, including knitted picks, knitters, wool and gang, knitted yarns, Amazon, and Etsy, in addition to your local specialty yarn store. Just experiment and have fun!

8. DOWELS

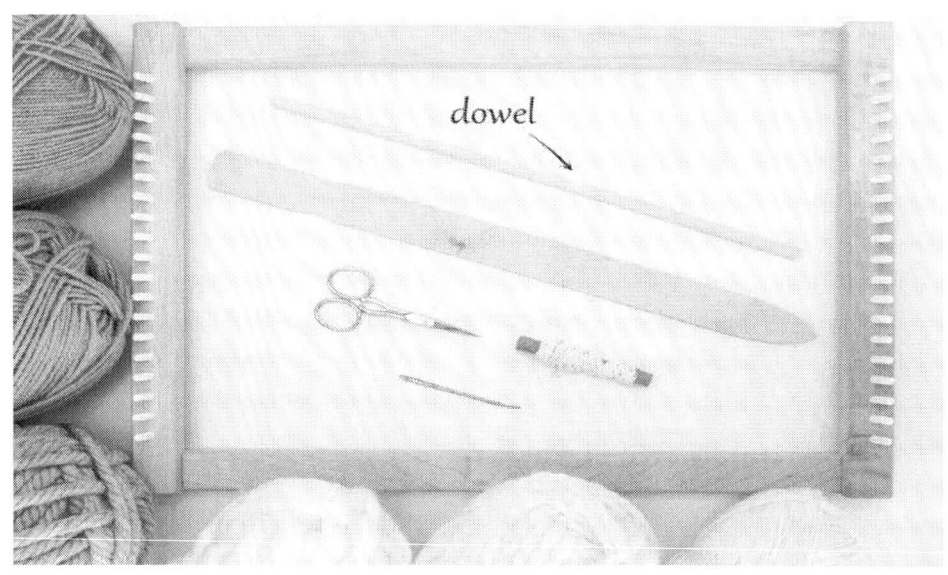

Unfinished wood

When you are ready to remove your texture from the loom, you will need a pin to fill the lines on top:

For wall weaving, the most dowel today is a wooden dowel, which is often not ready to make the texture stand out. You can buy them in bulk on Amazon and then cut them to size (at least 2-4 inches wider than your texture). Or you can buy a small package like this.

Other varieties

Don't limit yourself to unfinished wood. There are so many other dowels to choose from on Etsy, including brass and driftwood.

And if you want to experiment, use decorative strands, embroidery rings, or even try lucite dowels to enhance your style. You can find any of these products at any of the online craft shops mentioned in the post.

CHAPTER ONE

TYPES OF LOOMS

So you've decided you want to capture the texture! A loom is the first thing you'll need. Here are some different looms and tips for choosing your first loom.

The loom holds the longitudinal threads tightly while other threads are woven through them. There are many various types of looms available, each with its own set of features, but they all do the same thing.

Once you understand the weaving process, it is easier to recognize the different types of looms, you need to better understand the weaving process. The threads held tightly on the loom are called warps, and the threads that cross the chain are called wefts.

WEAVING AND LOOM BASICS

During the weaving process, the weave raises or lowers a portion of the warp fibers to form an opening. The texture pushes the weft out of the opening with a device called a shuttle. Except for the simplest looms, such as frame weaves, all looms can produce sheds in some fashion. For example, on axial looms, warp fibers are lifted or lowered because they hang from straps that hang on frames called straps. When the weave raises or lowers the straps with the tread or arms, the warp threads projected on these straps go up or down and a shed is created. On simpler looms (ink looms, back looms, and rigid hedge looms), the foundations are manually moved up or down to create the barn.

Weft transfer can be as simple as a screw rod, or it can be a fairly technical air transfer that enlarges the weft with a fast movement of the cord. When a shuttle passes the lead through the wall of the chain, it leaves a weft mark. Each passage through the shed is called a pickaxe. After each pick, the texture changes the barn by changing which warp is raised or lowered and uses a part of the loom called a reed that resembles a very large comb in the frame. Pickaxe placement is called beating, although except in the case of heavy carpeting, placement is best described.

The wicker determines the distance of the warp yarns along with the beat so that the resulting fabric is evenly woven. The loom of the strap and the ink depending on the natural tendency of the fibers to move together rather than at the distance of the reed, and use the transfer edge to beat. Create the shed, take up space between the warp threads, and beat the warp threads on the stiff hedge loom, which also contains hedges and reeds.

TYPES OF LOOMS
1. BACKSTRAP LOOM

The back loom is a simple loom invented by ancient civilizations that is still in use today in many places. The chain is tied around an object at one end and attached to the texture at the other end. The weight of the texture keeps the chain tight. Informed weaves can produce beautiful and complex patterns using back looms.

2. TAPESTRY LOOMS

The tapestry loom contains the simplest loom, the frame loom.

Weaving the frame is not able to create a shed, and the upholstery created on the canvas is limited to the size of the frame. Some larger types of tapestry loom contain longer warp threads and offer methods for creating a shed.

3. INKLE LOOMS

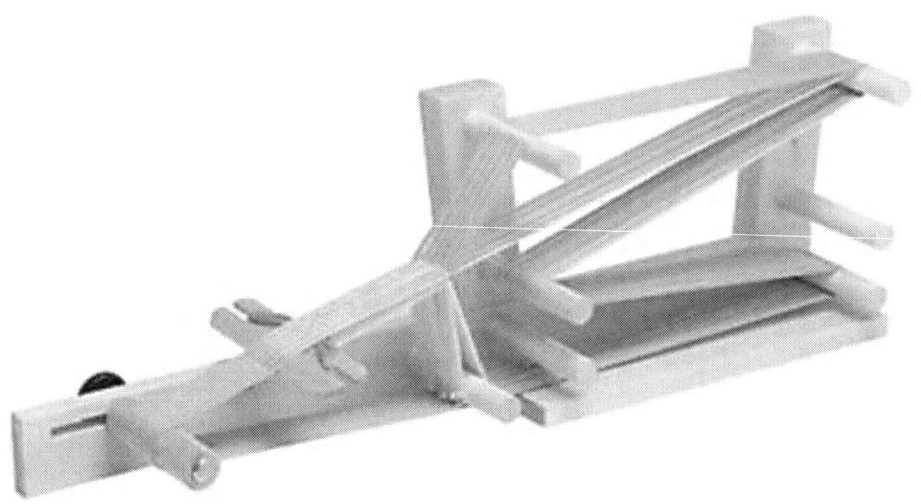

Narrow strips of fabric, such as straps and belts, are woven with ink textiles. They are portable, and while they are good for beginner looms, experienced weavers also use them to create complex patterns.

4. RIGID HEDDLE LOOMS

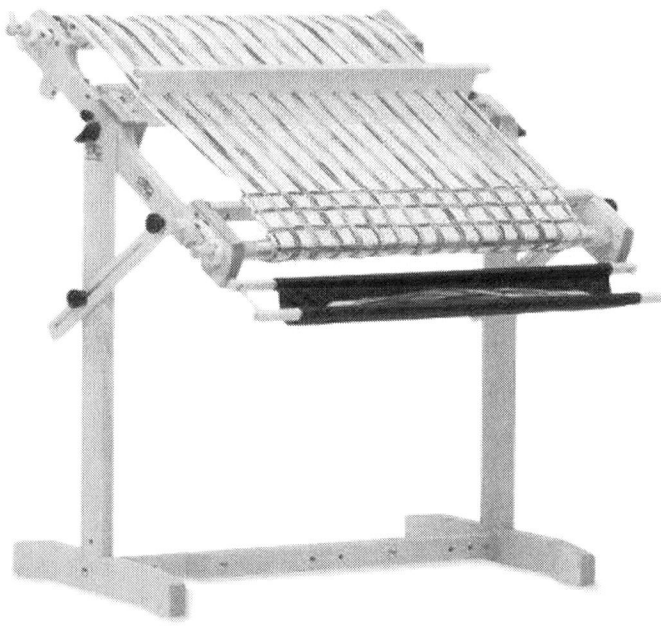

A rigid hedge loom is a good loom for a beginner. It offers a lot to experienced weavers by manually manipulating the chain and weft. With rigid weave, yarns that are generally thicker than those with axial looms can be used for biaxial weaving. With the addition of another hedge, the weave can use thinner yarns and weave more complex patterns with sticks and manual manipulation techniques. The rigid hedge loom is portable. It's possible to use it with or without a stand.

5. TABLE LOOM

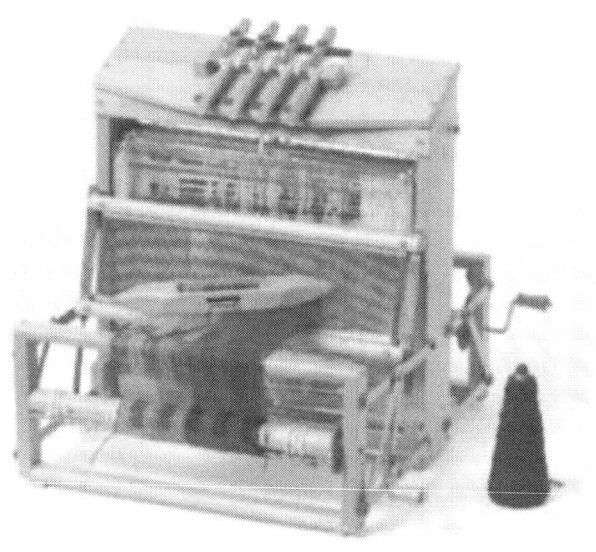

Table looms are more intricate than the other micro looms on our list, but they are smaller and more portable than floor looms. They are designed for use on a table or stand. Although you can get a table loom that has more than 8 axes, the most common types are 4 or 8.

6. FLOOR LOOMS

These are the largest of the loom looms of the house. They are stand-alone and made for weaving larger projects. Use floor tape to make longer and wider pieces of fabric, homemade bedding, accessories, and rugs. Floor tapes usually have 4 or 8 axes, but there may be more. It can also be electronically controlled by a cylinder that raises and lowers the harness to create sheds.

WHAT TO CONSIDER WHEN BUYING A LOOM

Before purchasing a loom, you should ask yourself a few questions.

1. What is your ability? Are you a seasoned weaver or just getting started? If you're not sure if weaving is a hobby or not, you can try a small loom first, such as a rigid hedge, ink, or table loom.
2. What kind of fabric do you want to make? If you are interested in upholstery, then a larger upholstery frame or loom is an obvious choice. If you are interested in making large pieces, floor texture is the best choice. If you don't mind making big pieces, any loom would be right for you. You can forget a lot of small pieces on large looms. If you want to make complex weaving patterns, floor or table looms with 4-8 axes are the best choice. Ink looms are the only option if you want to weave ribbons and belts.
3. How much space is available for looms and equipment? Floor fabric can have a very large mark, while some other looms are quite small and can be placed while in use. Floor tapes and table looms also require other equipment, such as warp and wind spool boards, that are not required by other looms.

The first aspect you want to do is the level of weaving ability. Are you a seasoned weaver or just getting started? If you're not sure if weaving will remain a hobby for you, start with a modest loom. If you already know you enjoy weaving, a large upright middle or even a more complex table loom may be a better investment.

Another aspect is what fabric you want to produce on your loom. What size do you want to produce? If you don't mind making large pieces, you may prefer an ink cloth or tapestry loom. If you're trying to create large or elaborate pieces, you're sure to need four-wire looms or upright looms.

Ink and stiff hedge looms are fantastic looms to start with if you want a little more functionality than a frame test. They are also good for children. Both looms are easy to learn and fun to use. Step up are four-axis table looms. They are more complex but portable. Finally, the serious weave should choose the weaving of the floor if there is room, or an eight-axis table loom if there is none. These looms are capable of producing intricate weaving patterns.

CHAPTER TWO

WEAVING TERMS

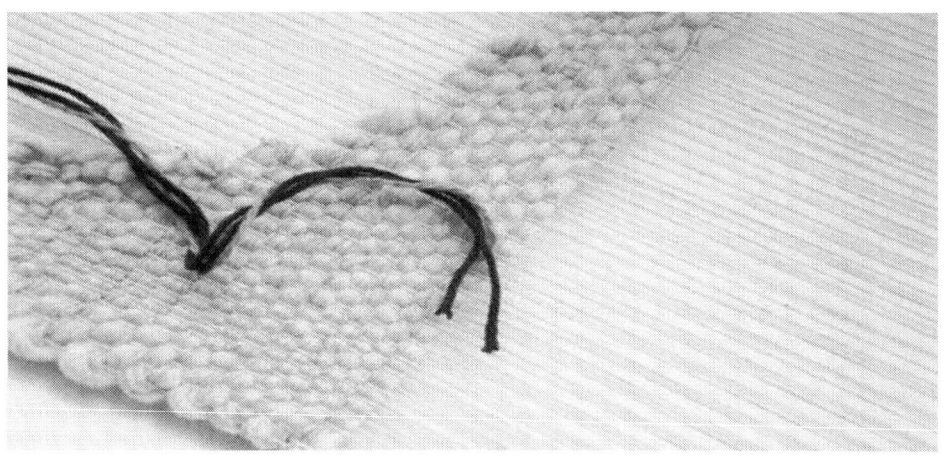

If you're new to weaving, some of the terminology can be bewildering at first. Here are some crucial terms to be aware of:

Frame Loom | The weaving loom

1. **loom**: loom is the structure you use to provide support and tension to your weaving during your work. Once its weaving is completed, it is cut from the loom and its weaving has its structure. The shape and size of the loom can vary greatly. From the extremely large floor model to the small handloom. The looms I use are frame textiles, which means they have a very basic, square or rectangular construction. Circular looms are also available, which allow the user to weave in a circle.

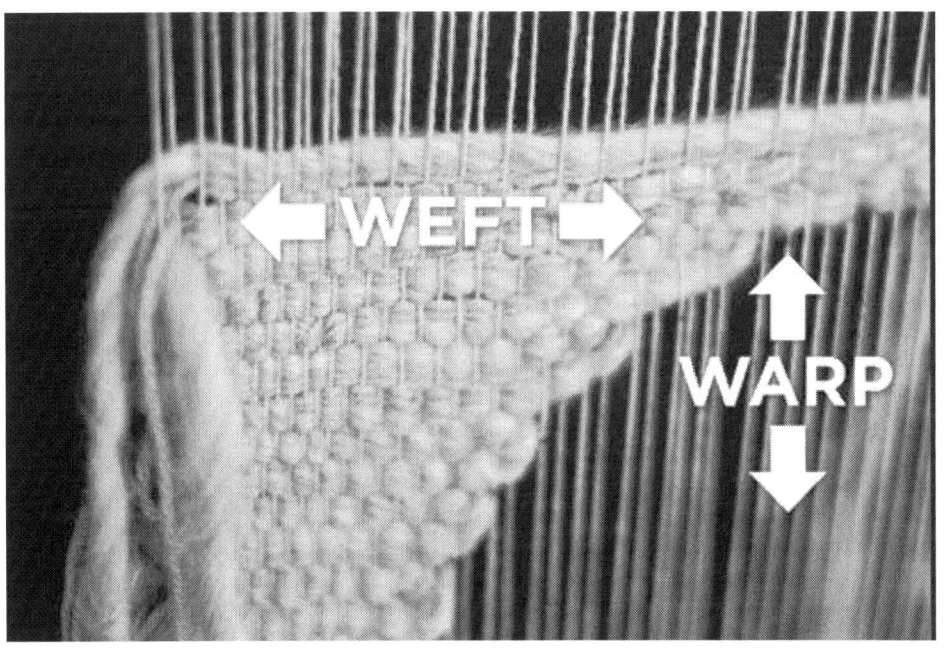

Warp and weft

2. **Warp thread**: This is the thread that is strung vertically on the loom and maintains tension as it is woven.
3. **Weft Yarn**: This is the fiber woven between the warp fibers, which creates patterns and structure in the weave.

Warp Shed

4. **Shed**: This separation of the warp yarns creates the upper and lower warp sets through which the weft thread passes. Creating a shed between the warp threads speeds up weaving. If a frame loom is used, a nest loom can be woven between the warp threads and then turned to the side to create a shed between the warp threads. Some frame texts come with a rotating eagle to create the barn.
5. **Heddle**: This creates a nest in the warp threads with the loom. To do this, the individual warp yarns are passed through the hedge so that the warp yarns can be separated while the weaving is running. The yarns may be rotating rods having grooves for warp yarns, or wires and cords separating warp yarns, or a rigid one-piece hedge having splits that either pull the warp yarns above or below the shed.

YARN FIBERS

The yarns used for knitting or crocheting are made of natural or synthetic fibers. Different yarns have special properties - some that are good, some that are not so good. Often, manufacturers mix different yarns to counteract unwanted properties.

When choosing a wall type, consider the following:

- **Wool**: Wool (made from sheep wool) is the queen of yarn and remains a popular choice for knitters. Here are some wool yarn options:
  - **Lamb's wool**: It comes from the first cutting of a lamb.
  - **Merino Wool**: It is considered the finest of the fine varieties.
  - **New pure wool / virgin wool**: Wool made directly from animal wool and not recycled from existing woolen clothing.
  - **Shetland Wool**: Made from small, hardy native sheep of the Shetland Islands in Scotland.
  - **Icelandic wool**: Soft and rustic yarn.
  - **Washable wool**: Chemically or electronically treated to destroy the outer layer of blurred fiber.
- **Fleece:** Mohair and cashmere from Angora and Kashmir goats are examples. Angora is derived from the fur of angora rabbits.
- **Silk, cotton, linen, and rayon**: Threads that are slippery, smooth, and often shiny.
- **Synthetic**: Nylon, acrylic, and polyester as well. Soybeans, bamboo, wheat, and other unique yarns are manufactured from plant-based materials that cross natural and manmade boundaries.

- ➢ **Novelty**: New yarns are easy to recognize because they look so different from traditional yarns:
  - **Ribbon**: knitted tape in rayon or rayon blend.
  - **Bouclé**: This very bumpy, woven yarn consists of loops.
  - **Chenille**: Although complex to work with, this thread has an attractive appearance and velvety texture.
  - **Thick-thin**: Thick and thin sections alternate, giving the knitted fabric a bumpy appearance.
  - **Railroad ribbon**: Small threads are "strung" between two parallel threads.
  - **Faux fur**: When knitted, the fluffy strands on strong nylon threads resemble faux fur.

Some new yarns are complicated to work with. Others can be very difficult. In strong seamless yarns, stitches are difficult, if not impossible, to identify, making them difficult to correct or sew.

- ➢ **Special feature**: These types of traditional yarns give a special appearance to knitted products:
  - **Tweed**: The background color is cracked with pieces of fiber of different colors.
  - **Heather**: She mixes several different colors or dyed wool and then turns it over.

- **Marled (ragg)**: Layered yarns in which the layers are of different colors.
- **Multicolored**: Painted in many colors or shades of one color.

YARN WEIGHT

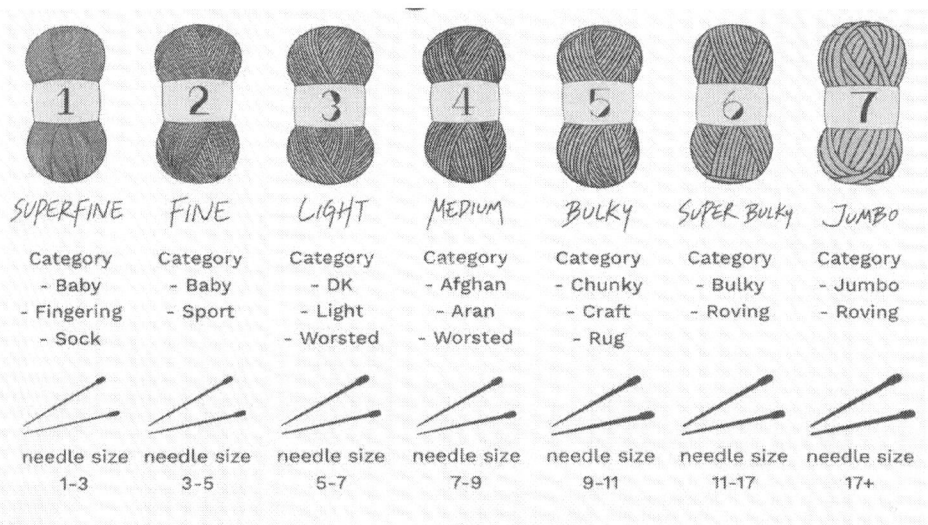

When you walk into a wall or craft shop, you are easily overwhelmed with all the options and don't know which wall is right for your project. Many people stick to the exact type of yarn (and even color) suggested in the pattern, but it's helpful to know how to set knitting instructions if you're pulling other types of yarn. While not every wall is perfect for every project, learning about the weight of the wall allows for much more creativity in your decisions.

THE STANDARD YARN WEIGHT SYSTEM

Wall weight refers to wall thickness. This is ranges from super fine to super voluminous. There are six different categories of thread weight, and the Craft Yarn Council says that certain thread weights should produce a somewhat predictable number of stitches when using a needle of a certain size.

The higher the number, the heavier the wall and the fewer stitches you get per inch, but the layer does not always correlate with the weight of a particular wall.

Why are standards important?

Knitting becomes fun here. If you know that each bulky thread gives about the same number of stitches (in this case 12-15 stitches in 4 inches on a 9-11 needle) and you have a pattern that uses bulky yarn and 10 needles, you can buy any bulky yarn and can get a similar result.

Of course, it is essential to tie a tape measure together before starting a scaling project, as not all yarns of a certain weight match exactly. The difference between 12 points every 4 inches and 15 points is still quite significant when trying to fit a sweater.

DETERMINATION OF YARN WEIGHT

Most yarn makers make determining the weight of a specific yarn simple. Most yarns produced in series use the standard yarn classification system, and the number and weight should be printed directly on the label.

Other manufacturers don't make it that simple, but they need to have measurements that say something like "24 stitches and 22 rows every 4 inches on size 4 needles". If you know a little about the weight of the wall (which you can find out by looking at the table below), then you know that the wall in question is a sport weight.

YARN WEIGHTS

If you still have trouble calculating the weight of the wall, craft store clerks should be able to answer any questions. You can also search the Internet for specific brand weights - most manufacturers provide this information.

CHAPTER THREE

HOW TO CHOOSE COORDINATIVE YARN COLORS

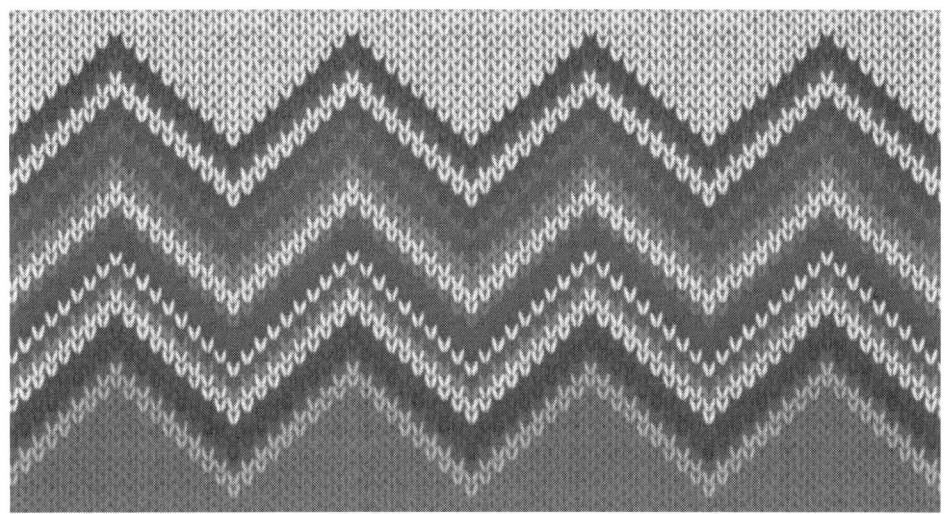

What if you wanted to work with a lot of colors and fibers, but didn't have a natural sense of color or formal art training? That was my situation. And I wanted to start trying to design my patterns and color palettes.

I was able to do the design, math, and schemes, but choosing more colors that I felt confident was going well was my hurdle. I always thought about what tools help knitters, and I was sure there were tools to help me choose the color.

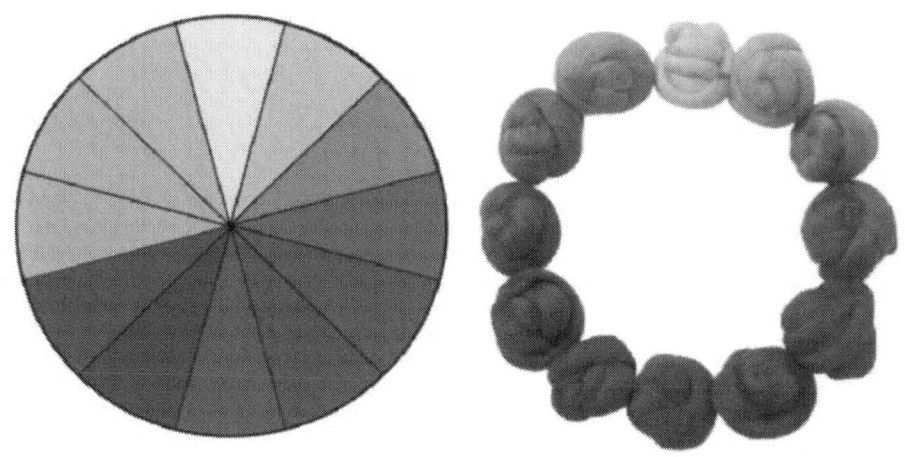

We all learned about the color wheel in high school, as part of the art class, but then it didn't make sense to me, and I was probably dreaming two lines on the boy instead of paying attention. So I bought a color bike and borrowed some books on the subject from the library. The books were interesting but were written by artists about painting. The paint can be changed by adding colors; wall no.

So I started my colorful adventure. I started by taking the two "harmonies" on the color wheel and the wall in hand (harmony is a pleasant relationship of colors) from two and I started doing color swatches. I wanted to see if I could start to make any sense of how using the color wheel can help knitters who have color impairment like me. Here are my findings:

1. A color wheel is a tool, and just like any new tool, you'll need to learn how to utilize it and how to take advantage of harmonies.

Most color bikes on the market have simple instructions. Start by knowing the terminology. The color wheel is the color spectrum that leans around. Shows the relationships between colors. Balanced and eye-catching color combinations are the harmonies I mentioned. To start using the color wheel for knitting or other fibrous crafts, select only one color and then create a palette that aligns that color by adding colors to the wheel according to the harmony of your choice.

2. For my design purposes, I found that I had to use only two of the color wheel - the triad and the split accessory.

The triad starts with three colors that are equidistant from the color wheel. It is represented by three gray triangles of the color wheel shown (Figure 1). Through these three colors, a fabric with high contrast is made because the colors are far apart on the wheel. The split-complementary harmony has two colors that are close together on the color wheel, but the third color is the opposite. It is represented by the three gray triangles (Figure 2). Because the main color and the second color are so close to each other, they create a fine contrast fabric; the third color, on the other side of the wheel, gives a large pop of contrasting color.

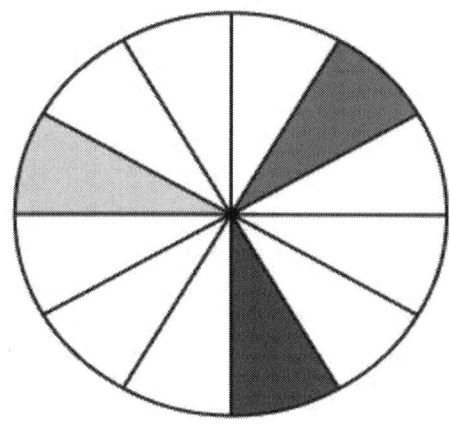

Figure 1 Triad – three colors equidistant from each other

Both harmonies work very well not only on color palettes but also on weaving and even choosing color combinations for the flower to brighten up the garden.

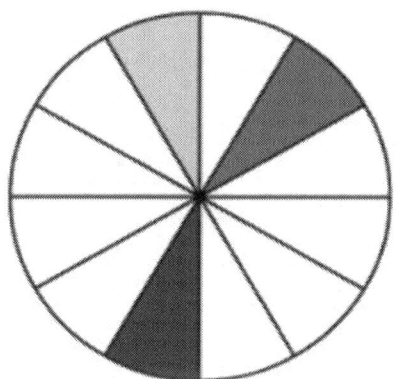

Figure 2

Split - one color and two colors that are on both sides of the complement.

3. If you use multiple colors, an odd number of colors works best. As an example, 3, 5, 7, 9, and so on. Observe point 5.
4. Proportion is important.

If you want the project to have a certain overall color, 50 percent of the wall you choose should be in that color, and 40 percent should be in the second position of the color wheel. Only 10 percent should come from the third position, which increases the contrast (Figures 3, 4, and 5).

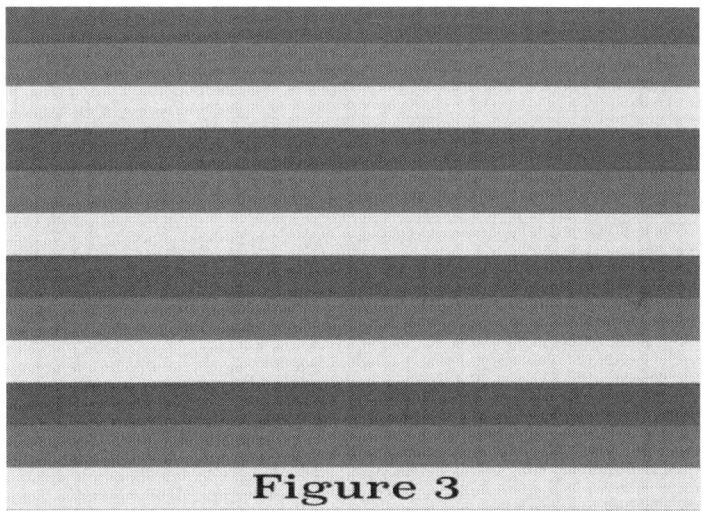

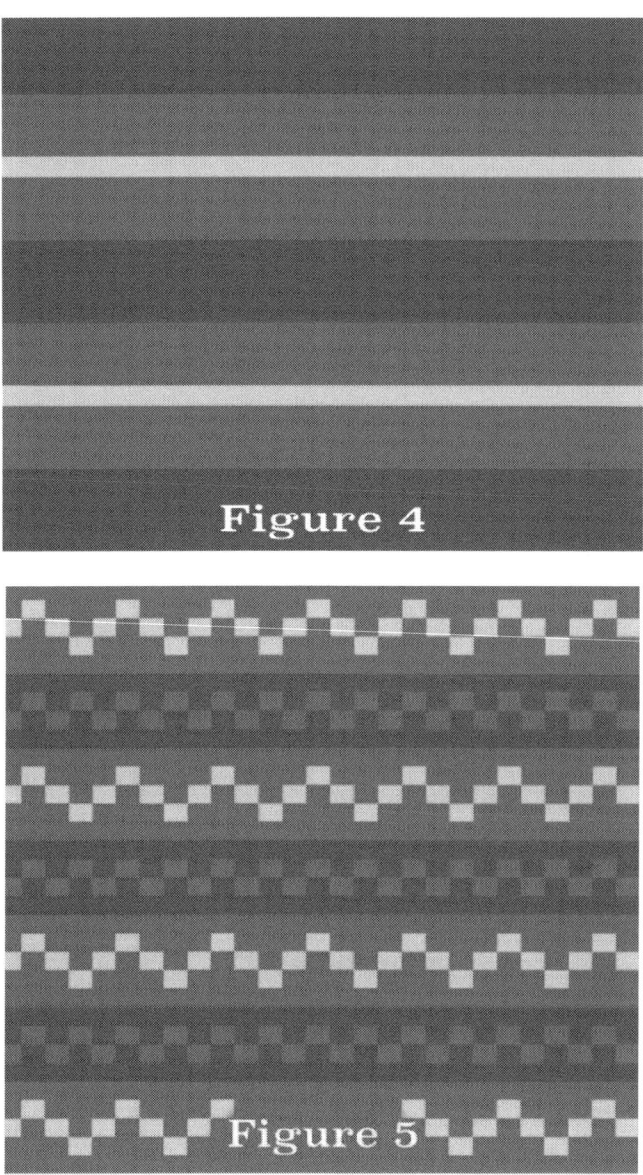

The fabric made from Figure 3 would be boring; Figure 4 is much more interesting. Even if there are only two yellow lines, these are obvious.

5. If you want to add to five colors, instead of adding different colors, change the value of the main and second current colors (make them lighter or darker).

This gives more interest to the tissue and maintains the 50/40/10 ratio (Figures 6 and 7).

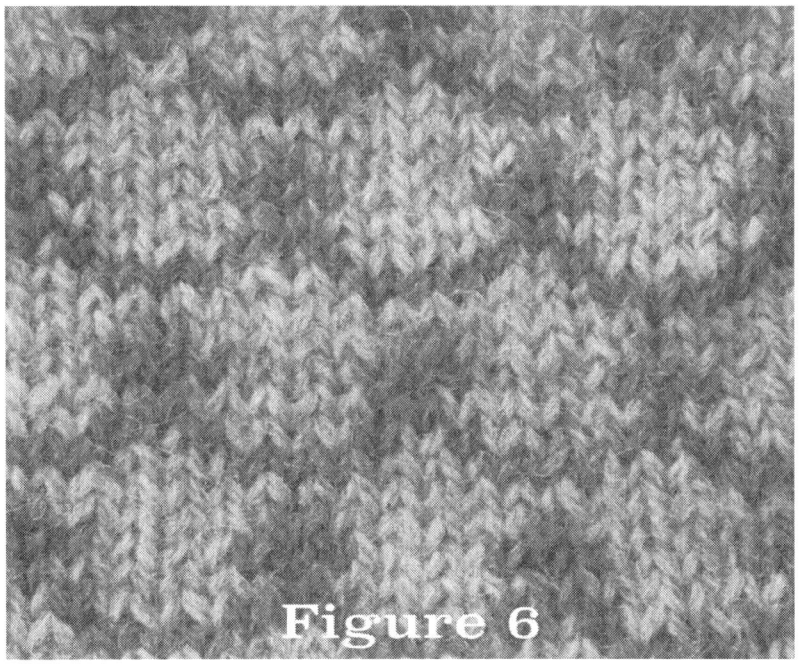

Figure 6

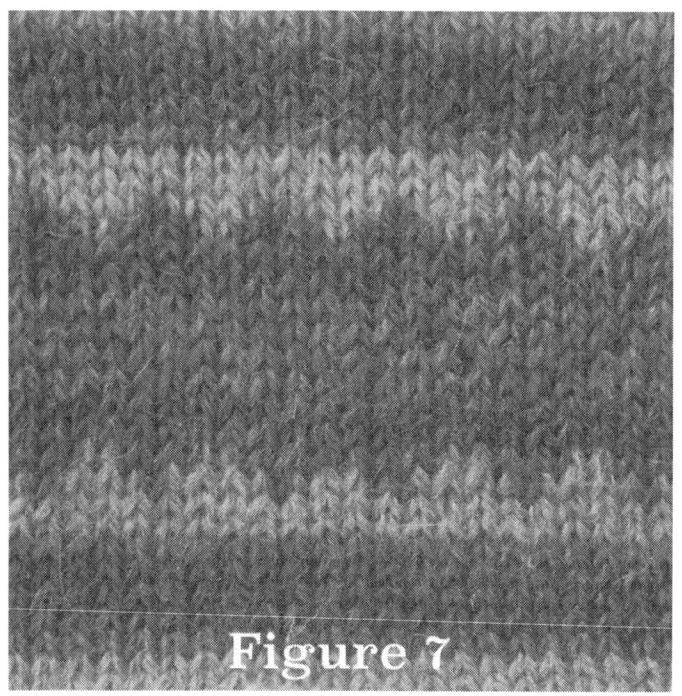

Figure 7

6. When working with stripes or markings, the value of the colors is less important, but a two-color twisted knit comes with a background design and foreground.

If there is not enough contrast in the value between the background and the colors of the foreground, the pattern will not be visible (Figure 8).

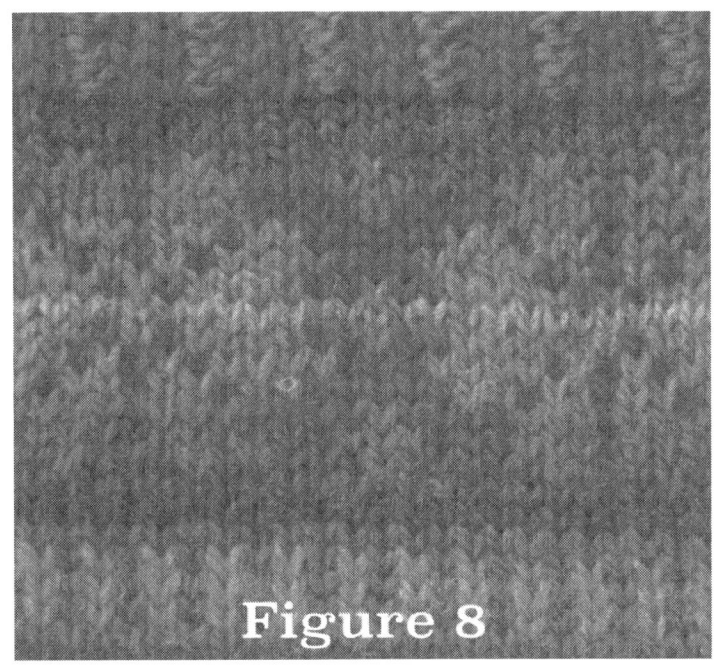

Figure 8

7. No wonder, the color wheel is neither black nor white.

I found that the best way to use either is to build my palette first and then replace black with one of the darker colors or white with the lighter ones. The use of black or white as a contrasting color is sometimes only necessary to achieve the desired effect. In two-color rounded work, black or white can be used as background or background (Figures 9 and 10).

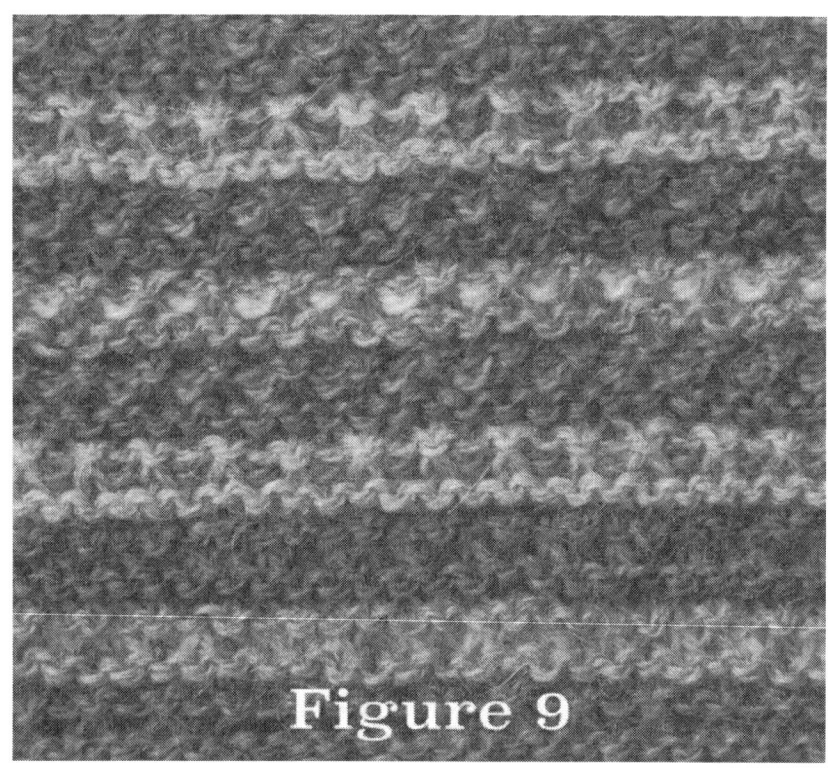

Figure 9

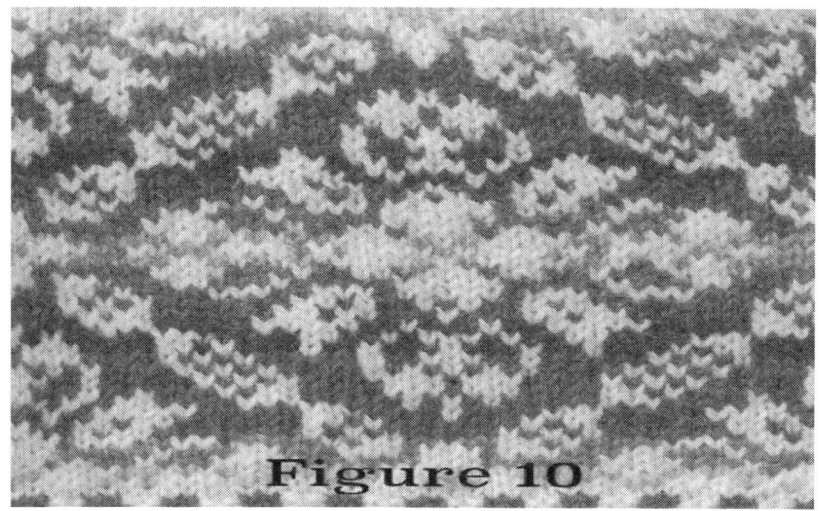

Figure 10

8. Brown appears on the color wheel is orange, red-orange, and red boxes.

When I build a color palette, I first choose between red and orange and then replace one with a brown one (Figure 11).

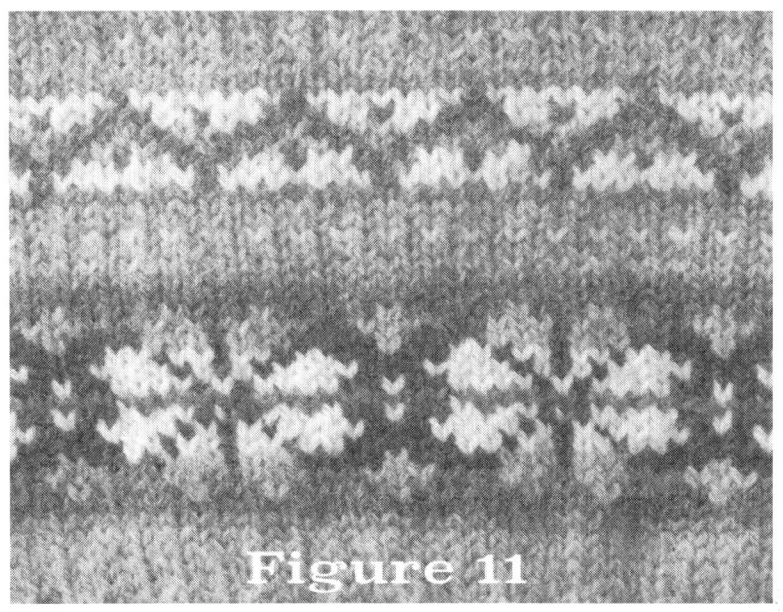

9. The need to bind the sample cannot be avoided.

Sometimes, even if the color choice is good, there is not enough contrast in the value. And sometimes a color swatch shows that color simply looks better elsewhere in design or graphics. Small adjustments can be made by reconnecting, not reconnecting (Figures 12 and 13).

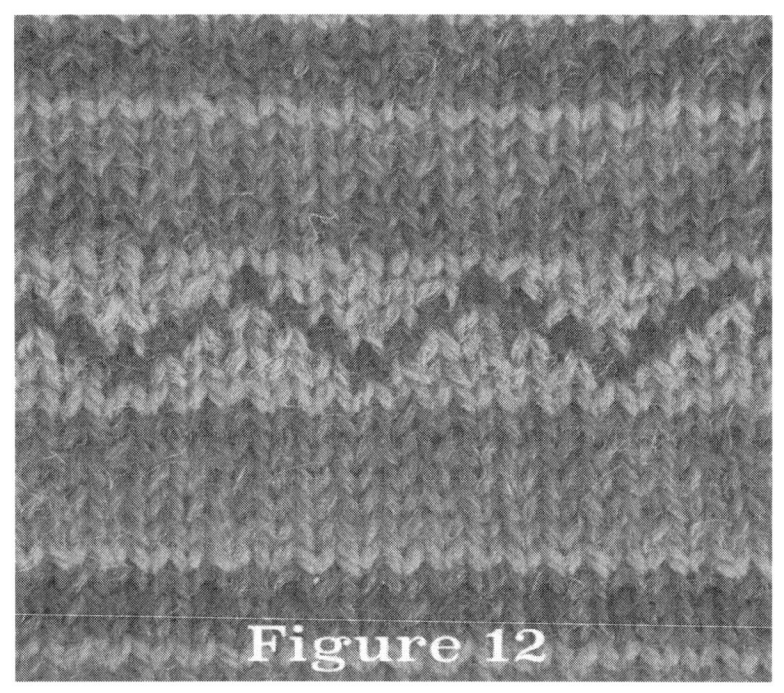

COLOR PALETTE CONSTRUCTION

If you want a high contrast fabric, choose Triassic harmony. If you want a finer color combination, choose a split and complementary harmony. Find a color you like first - just one. Compare the color of the color wheel. Rotate the top wheel until one point of the triangle or one of the short points of the split triangle accessory is on the color box that best fits your wall. Now follow the color wheel to select the other colors.

For three colors, the ratio would be 50 percent for your main color and 40 percent for one of the other three triple points, or the short side of the split supplement. Select a 10% contrast color from the triad's third point or the split compliment's long side.

For five colors, add more colors/interests by selecting a different value for the main color and the second color. For seven colors, add two contrasting colors. These colors are adjacent to the main and second colors of the color wheel and move to the first contrast color. In the triad, these two complement each other. And if we want to go for nine, just add another value to the main and second colors so that each has a light, medium, and dark value.

SELECTION OF WARP YARN

Understanding the good warp yarns or warp yarns used for weaving is basic knowledge for any weaver. The best weaving yarn depends on several factors. This post reviews some general rules and tips/tricks for choosing the best warp thread for your project.

STEP 1: Consider the type of weaving project

The textured design greatly influences the type of warp yarn required and the type of fibers selected.

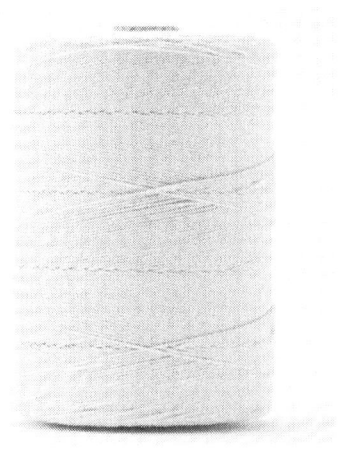

Cotton Seine twine

WARP YARN FOR TAPESTRY AND RUG WEAVING

For weaving tapestries, rugs, and other weft-facing weaving projects where you will beat your weft a lot, you need a very strong woolen yarn, linen, or cotton warp that is specifically kept under high tension.

A beam of organic cotton yarn

WARP YARNS FOR TOWELS, PLACEMATS, OR HOME TEXTILES

When weaving towels, tablecloths, or other household textiles, you must use a soft, solid yarn that can easily handle loom tension during bending, and that is machine washable and lasts for years.

Our Mallo, Duet and Beam yarn lines can be used both as yarns and as wefts in towels, tablecloths, and other household textiles.

Colored field virgin weaved with silk braid

WARP YARN FOR SCARVES, SHAWLS, OR APPAREL WEAVING

If you're making a wool, silk, or alpaca scarf, you probably won't beat it as much as upholstery or home fabric, then the wall shouldn't be stiff. However, this must still be strong enough to handle stress and wear in the shell, which is discussed below.

Our warp and weft yarns for weaving scarves, shawls, and other fabrics are made from black silk and alpaca.

Skyline towel weaving pattern

WARP YARN FOR A RIGID HEDDLE LOOM

When selecting warp yarns for rigid spinning looms, make sure the yarn is appropriate for your project as well as the size of your hedge. For example, thin yarns such as 8/2 cotton can only be used as a chain on a rigid hedge weave if the fibers are doubled and woven together, as in these Skyline towels. Suffolk wool-like thick yarns can be used on 7.5- or 8-hole hedges, but are too thick to work well on 12-hole hedges on rigid looms.

STEP 2: Consider the strength of the warp thread

It is important that the warped wall is strong enough to withstand the tension between the two beams and to handle the wear and tear from hedges and reeds when the shafts are moving and the weft is filled with a beater (floor or table loom) or elevator and lower the rigid reed of the hedge to create a loom (for rigid weaving of the hedge). However, it can't be so stretchy that you lose your tension.

THE SNAP TEST

The "Snap Test" is one of the most common methods for determining whether a thread is suitable for warping. Try to weave 6 "into your hands. If you don't tear - great - it will probably be a good warp yarn!

AN EXCEPTION TO THE SNAP TEST RULE

The linen yarn is very strong and generally does not burn, but it is famous for wearing and breaking during weaving. And many threads that do not pass the snap test are fantastic warp threads because the tension in a chain is spread over many lines, reducing the tension on one line.

Therefore, it is important to have a good and uniform tension on the chain. So here's a little finishing for snaps: if the wall breaks with a clean, clean, audible "snap," it's probably good for a warp thread as well. If it spreads quietly (as often happens in the case of soft one-layer braided yarns), it's probably not a good choice for warp yarns. In our warehouse, almost any wall is suitable for bending on the floor or a rigid hedge loom (if not, say that in the description).

STEP 3: Consider the number of threads in the warp threads

As a general rule, thick yarns (twisted yarns with multiple yarns) are easier to use for warp yarns because they are generally stronger and more balanced. But that doesn't mean no braided yarn can be used successfully!

Of course, the multilayer yarn should be sampled and strength tested to see if it is suitable for use as a warp yarn. Just because it sounds good on paper doesn't mean it will work - strength testing and sampling are always important!

YARNS RECOMMENDED FOR WARP AND WEFT

The following three yarns can be used for both warp and weft, regardless of whether they are woven on a rigid shield weave or a multi-axis loom.

1 BEAM ORGANIC COTTON

Organic cotton with beam

This 3/2 organic, unwoven cotton is soft, durable, and easy to start with for towels, home textiles, and clothing. Made from 100% organic cotton in the United States.

2 MALLO COTTON SLUB

Mallo cotton slub

Thick, thin cotton yarns designed for weaving soft, absorbent textiles, scarves, or household garments. Made in the USA from 100% cotton (55% organic).

3 COTTON DUET / LINING

Duet of cotton linen yarn

The versatile yarn, the Duet is strong enough for warp yarns, soft enough for clothes, and hard enough for kitchen clothes. Made in the US, 55% from European towels, and 45% from cotton produced in the US.

CHAPTER FOUR

WARP THE LOOM

What kind of loom do you have? I always wonder what other people's weaving is, especially when it comes to looms I've never seen before. Of all the looms available to me, I found that there are two basic ways of warping circular yarns. The first one is "S", the second is "8. Warping.

The most common ones I found are pins or ear looms. These looms are twisted "S" around the loom pegs or the tabs on the top and bottom of the loom.

HOW TO WARP DIFFERENT LAP LOOMS

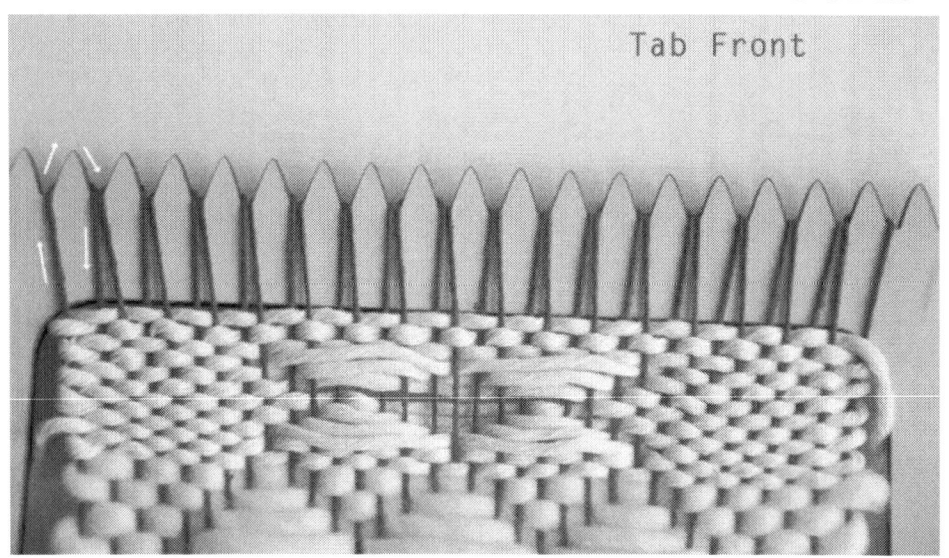

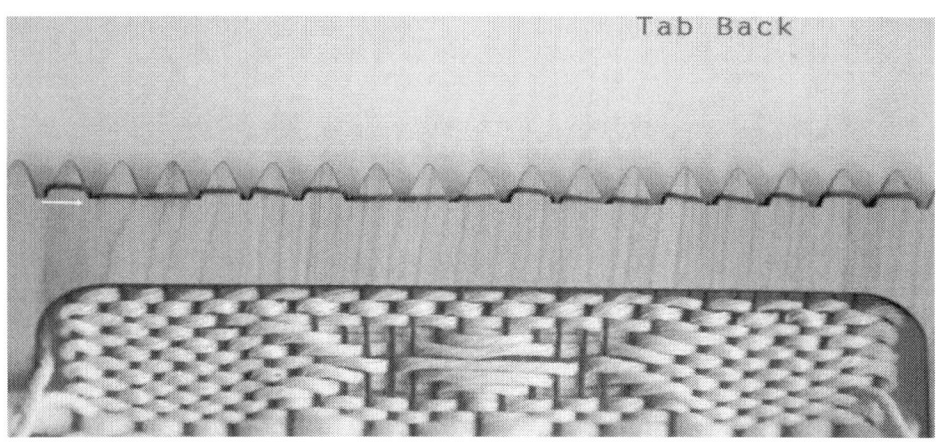

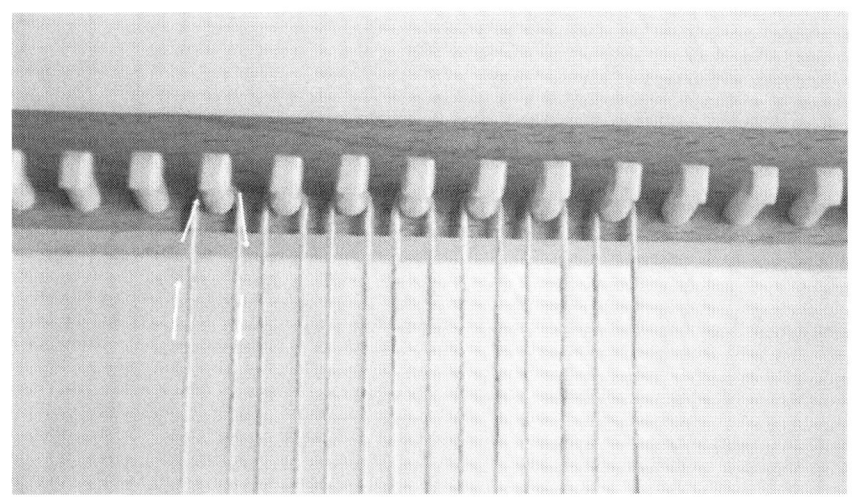

1. To bend these looms, I start in the lower-left corner and tie my warp thread to the pin frame, ear, or even the loom. Then apply the warp thread on the top nail/tab and move the warp thread around and back to that nail/tab. Guide the warp thread around the lower pin/tab and back. Repeat this until the loom is twisted.

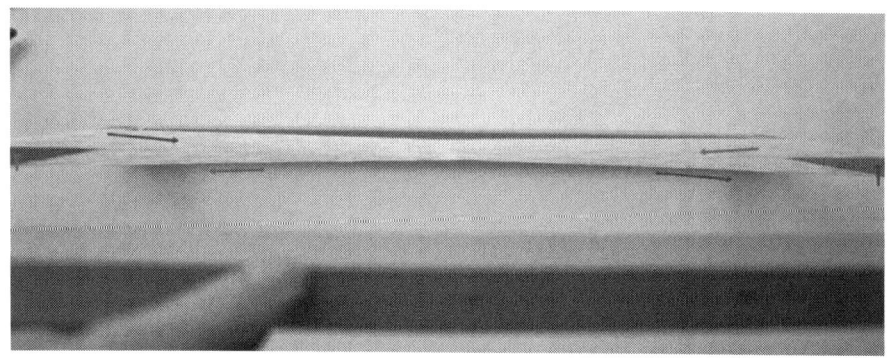

2 I call this way the "S" Warp because if you turn the loom side, you see that the chain makes "S" shapes from one nail/ear to another.

Another loom that weaves is a frame weave. It is a loom that is projected directly onto the loom frame. The best part of this warping technique is that you can forget a lot of things, like a picture frame, a tree branch, or anything else that has a strong texture.

These looms are warped "8 Way. For this, I tie the warp thread to the lower-left frame. Then apply the warp thread to the front and back of the frame. Then I take the chain down and in front and behind the frame. The warp thread always passes in front and behind the loom, causing the warp yarns to meet in the middle to form Figure 8. This is very useful when weaving on a frame because it brings out the warp together in the middle and makes it much easier. All these warp fibers are used in weaving. It is here in much more detail.

TABBY WEAVE

weft threads

warp threads

Tabby weaving is the simplest knitting system. It is based on two or more warp fibers (ends) and two or more weft fibers (picks). All weft yarns across the warp yarns and under them. The next weft thread then goes below and above the warp threads. The third weft thread repeats its first operation, goes above and below, and so on.

Weaving a balanced tabby, where there is an equal number of yarns per square centimeter in the chain and weft.

Also known as weaving; plain fabric; smooth weaving; smooth weaving.

RYA KNOT

Rya knots are often found at the bottom of the weave to create fringes. The rya knot, on the other hand, can be used to produce a more unique and intriguing composition. These knots are also used when making a shaggy carpet weave because the knot holds the ends of the fiber in place.

I wove it from top to bottom, so I put the knots of my rya upside down. However, there are many weavers I know from the bottom up.

I suggest always making a few simple weave lines to ensure the stability of rya knots. In this example, I start from the bottom up.

I supported three rows of simple textures. Then I added the knots of my rya. In my example, I used four strands of combed weight to get an average thickness (here you can learn more about wall weight). To create a rya knot, you must use at least two warp threads for each knot.

I used four warp yarns (two on each side) as I make a medium knot. The number of warp threads taken affects the width of the rya knots. If you are making a wider rya knot, you will need a thicker amount of thread or more yarn, otherwise, the rya knot may be loose.

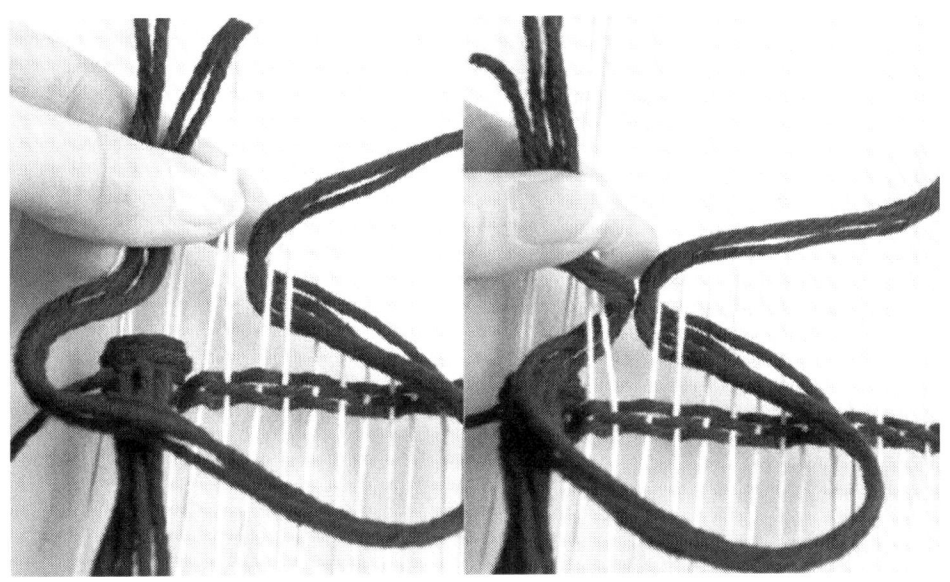

Rya Knot1

STEPS TO CREATE RYA KNOTS:

Step 1

I put my four threads on the warp thread.

Step 2

Take the right side of your yarn behind and around your warp yarn (in my example, I go around two warp yarns. Then wrap the left side of your yarn around the yarn of the other warp, bringing the ends together in the middle.

Rya Knot

Step 3

Since we start with rya knots (weaving from the bottom up), the edge pieces are pulled under the top area of the knot. If the rya ends with knots (weaving from top to bottom), pull the edge pieces over the top area of the knot.

Quick hint: Join both sides of the edge pieces and pull equally so that my knot with all the ends is around before removing the ends and tightening the top knot. Smooth fringes usually require cutting, but this helps prevent so many threads from loosening.

After adding the rya knot row, I suggest forgetting at least two rows of the simple weave to stabilize the knots. You can then make the other pieces as you wish. It is also possible to list another node rya.

As always, I recommend that you experiment until you discover the right amount of thread and knot size for you. This can also vary depending on which piece you are working on.

In one of my previous braids, I missed adding rows of support under my rya knots and had to tie crazy warp threads (see picture below) to get stability in my weave after I cut it from the weave. . Believe me you don't want to do that, we learned the lessons!

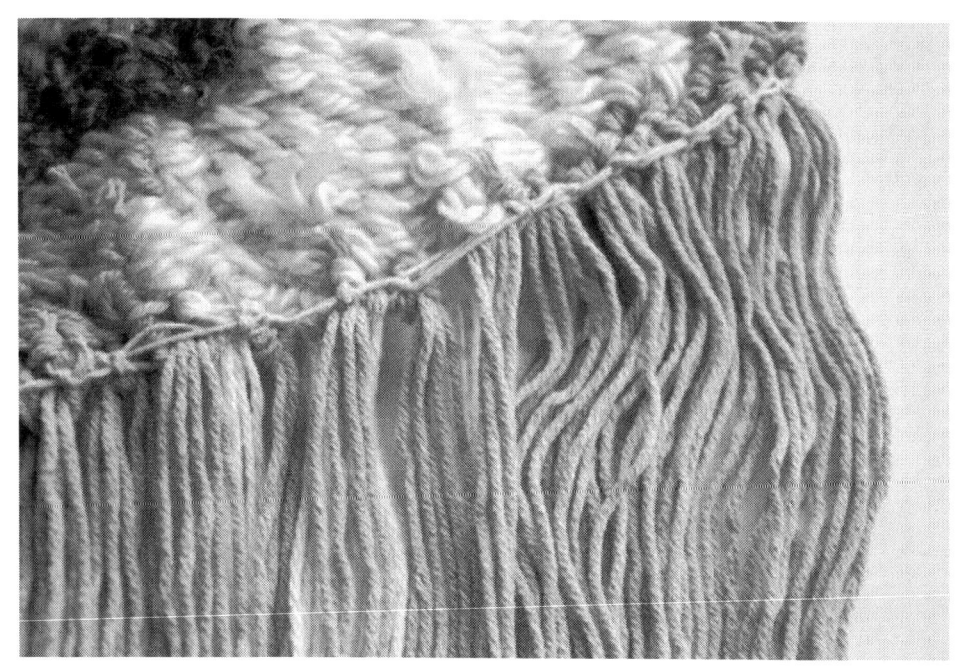

Rya Knot

CHAPTER FIVE

WEAVING SHAPES

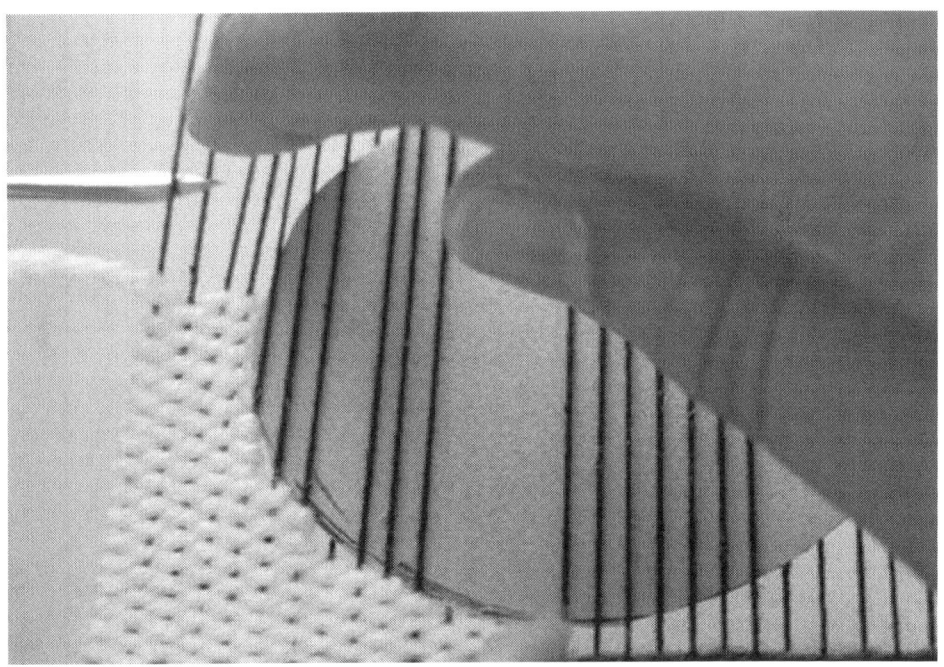

I hope you took a lot of time weaving. Once you get used to the patterns and use of the loom, it will be much easier to relax and be creative!

To learn how to forget shapes, you need to have a basic understanding of simple weaving. (You can learn simple weaving here in this previous post,

As it shapes between woven patterns and changing colors, this scenario weaves. You need to know how to change colors and restart and stop patterns. To do this, you must know one of the following methods:

- ➤ Weft entanglement, relieving weaving imperfections
- ➤ Warp woven fabrics weave both weft yarns and warp yarns.
- ➤ Leave a gap between the weft threads by forgetting the gaps

HOW TO WEAVE A CIRCLE

Circular weaving requires practice to create the type of curve desired. The woven ring can be curved with crisp edges and more geometrically with edges in a box - but one thing is for sure, it will take a lot of practice to make the desired ring look.

There are two methods I will follow in this tutorial: cut a circular shape or draw and follow a circular pattern on paper.

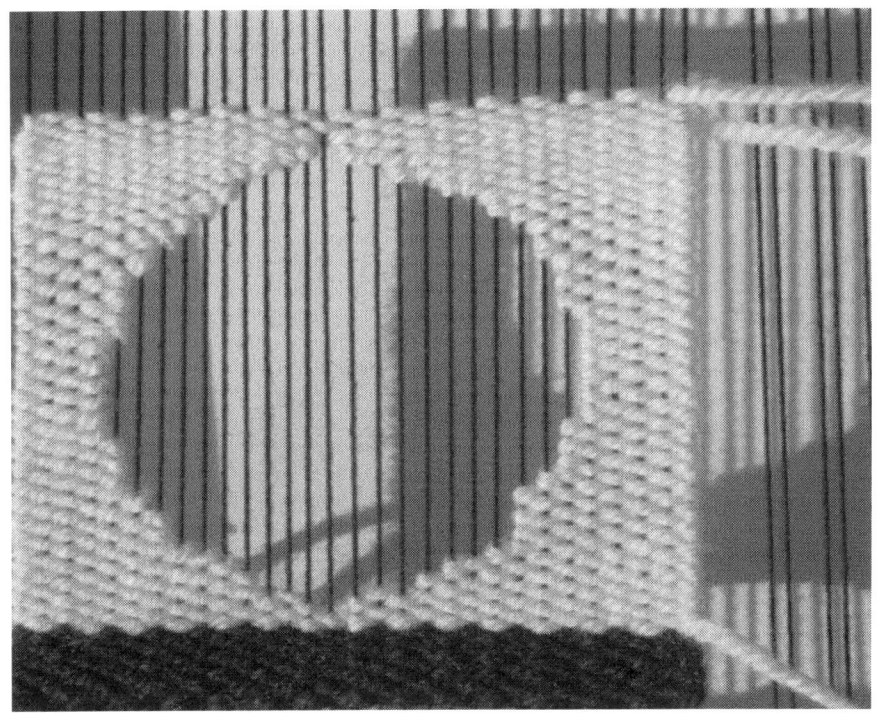

Spinning ring shapes

HOW TO WEAVE A RECTANGLE

Rectangles are as simple as plain weaving and can be set to square or other shapes.

Rectangle texture shapes

HOW TO WEAVE A TRIANGLE

Once you have learned how to weave a triangle, you can add them as borders, or play with their rotation and size to create a pattern.

Triangle weaving shapes

Conclusion

Adding shapes and images adds design, color, and movement to your texture. Experimenting with the size, color, and texture of shapes can also bring pictures to life.

CREATE BLOCKS USING A STRAIGHT SLIT

Weft warp and weft are techniques used to add color blocks and create color seams. In these techniques, two weft yarns are woven or bonded to the warp yarns.

Weaving gaps between color blocks is another weaving technique used to add colors side by side. This technique creates clear dividing lines between the weft thread and the warp thread.

In this tutorial, you will learn the technique of weaving gaps. Woven gaps are common

Create colored blocks in which 2 weft threads are not connected. When you forget two colors in the same row and reach the desired length with one color, the thread is sent back to create a new row.

WEAVING SLITS

This tutorial starts with a triangle. If you want to start with the same shape or a different shape, you can find a complete tutorial here in this blog post: Weaving Weaving in the Loom Guide.

First step:

Weave a smooth row next to the section from which you will weave a blank.

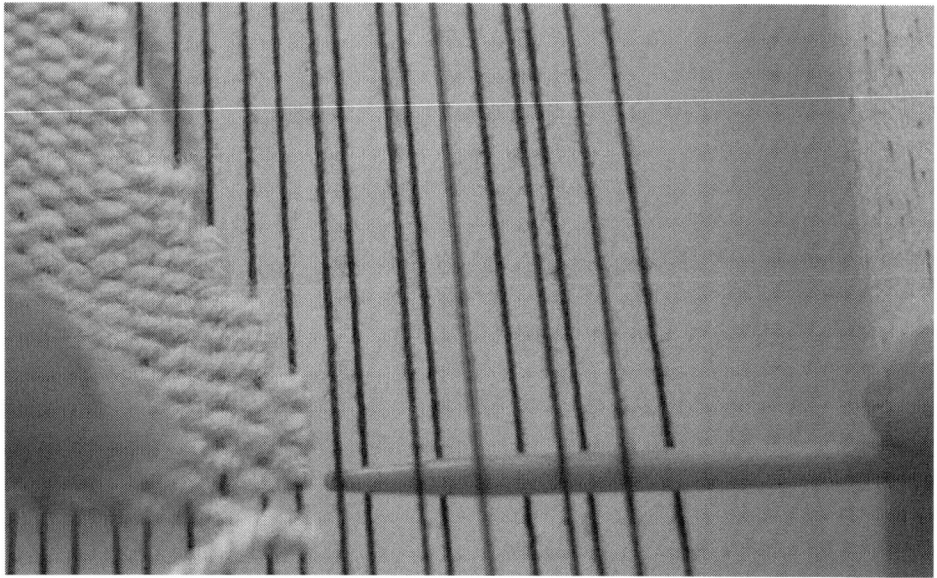

Weave until the warp yarn is reached before beginning the next set of weaving.

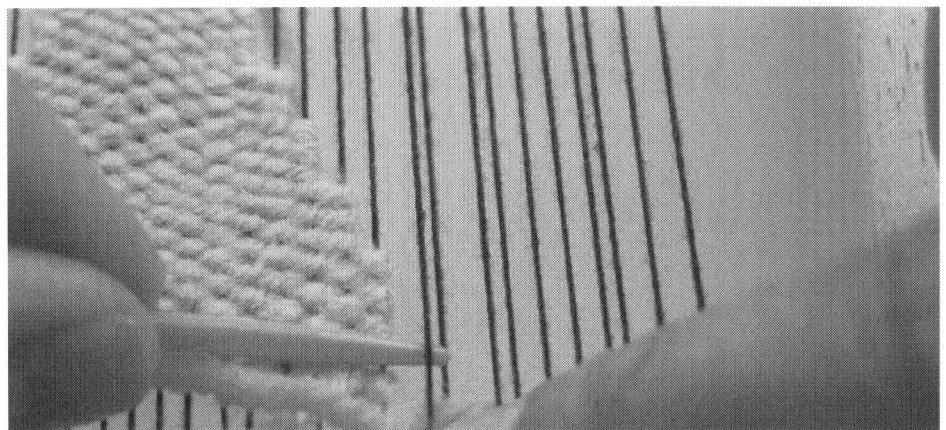

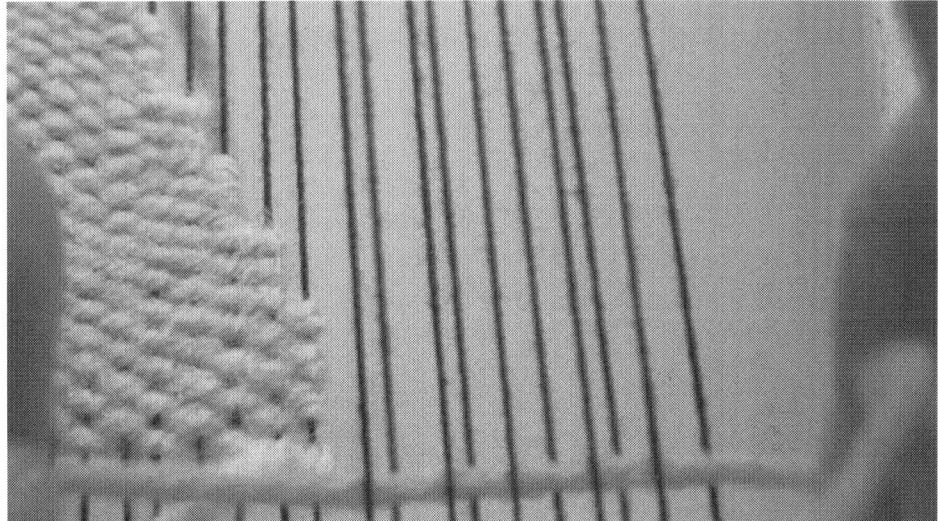

Step 2:

Weave a row back and secure the weft thread with a petticoat or loom fork.

Continue to do this until it reaches the desired height. In this tutorial, the model travels every 3 rows of weft and advances after the three rows.

Note: The two threads never connect, so there should always be an opening between them.

Tips: Be sure to adjust the tension between the two weft threads and the chain. Avoid pulling the chain too far to keep it straight.

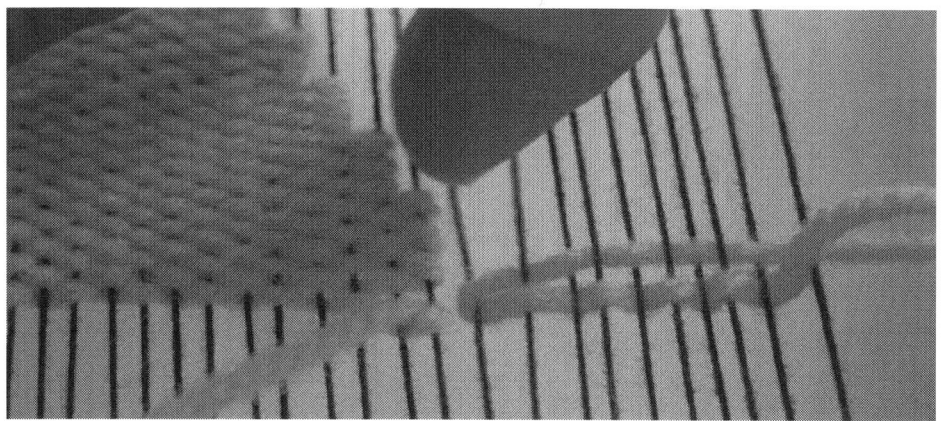

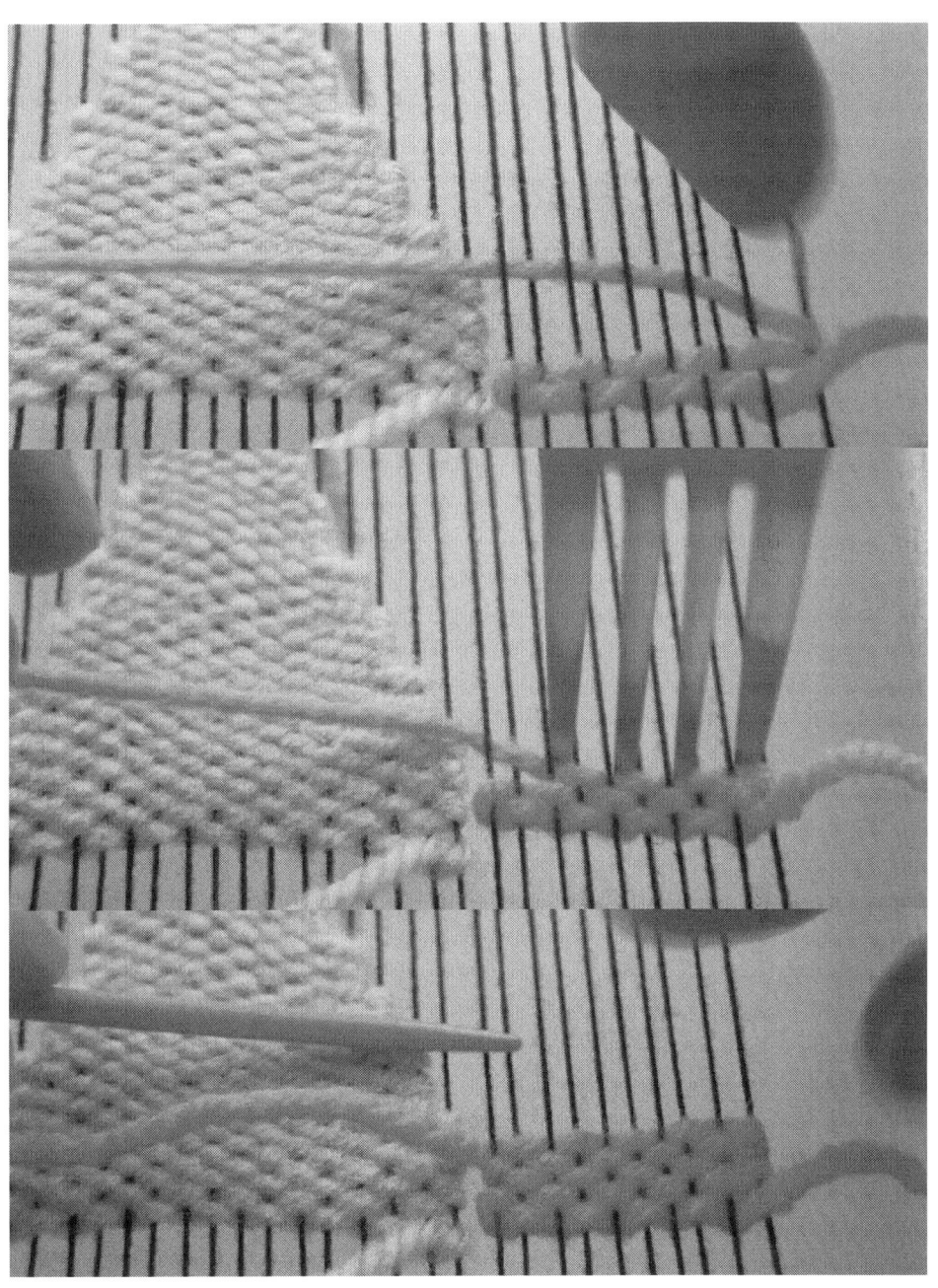

Weaving slits weaving techniques

Step 3:

Now the three rows are woven. It fits the pattern on the up texture.

To the left of the triangle is an inward pattern for each triangle. Therefore, the right weft thread should follow this pattern. However, you must move forward in three rows to stand next to the triangle.

The next row of orange weft threads runs a warp thread forward.

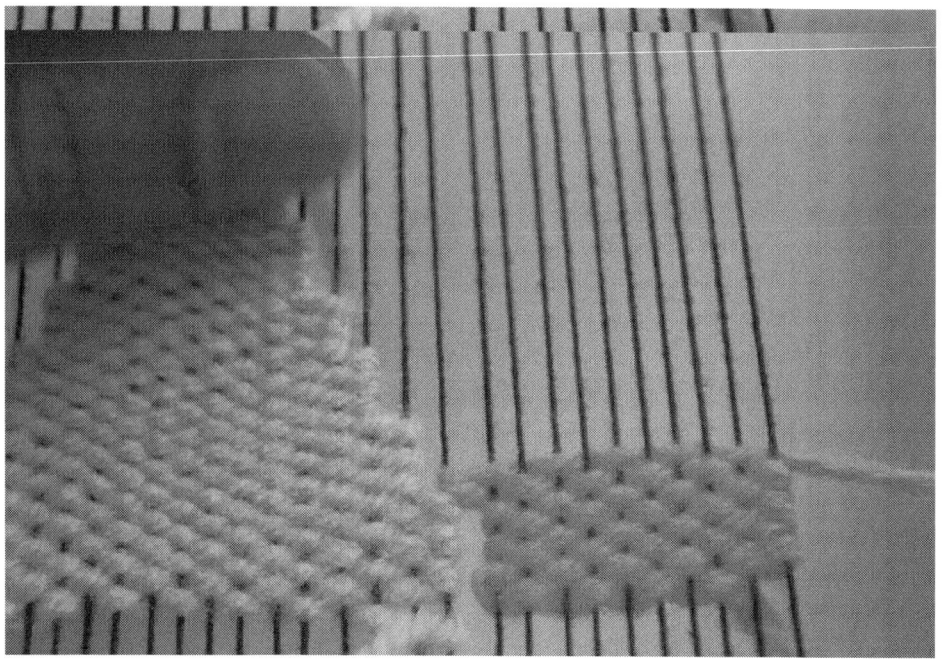

Continue to build the weft to fit the same height of the triangle or shape to the left.

STEP 5:

Continue with one weft thread one row forward and the preceding stages until the pattern is complete.

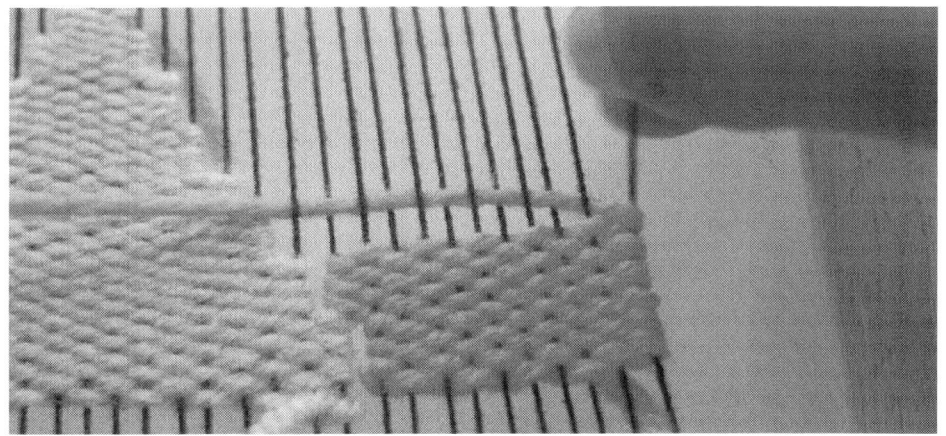

Check that a slit has been created.

Weaving techniques of weaving gaps

Below is a picture of weaving the slots on the right and the chain locking method on the left. Check out the blog post Weave Slits: Weaving Techniques to discover how to do this way on the left.

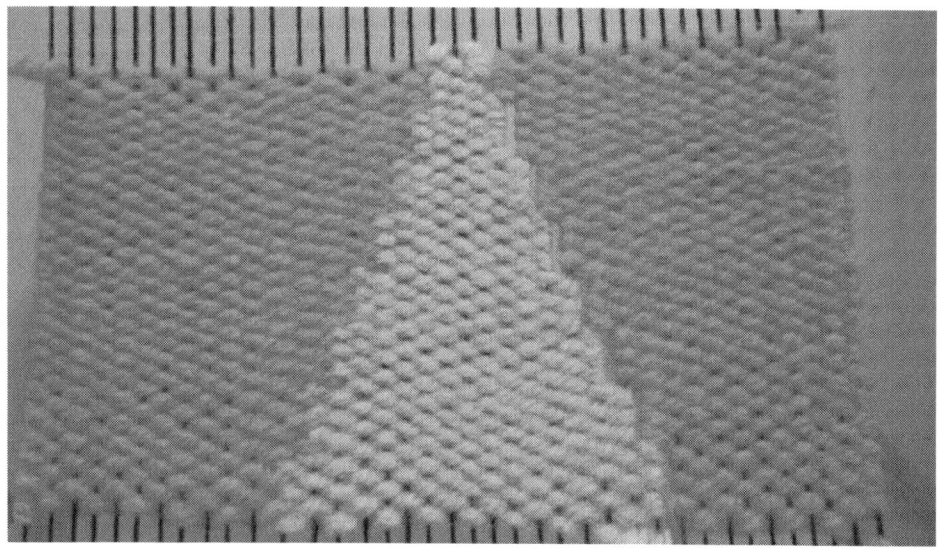

Weaving techniques

Conclusion:

In this tutorial, I learned the technique of weaving gaps.

There are a variety of strategies for weaving colors and creating compositions, so choose the one that best suits your weaving needs. It takes time and practice.

Over time, I enjoyed weaving the gaps between the colored blocks. I love the clean lines it creates between colors. However, if the blocks are too high, the stability of the threads may be impaired. As a result, I try not to weave these portions too high or to secure the sections with a wall between the colored blocks.

CHAPTER SIX

SOUMAK WEAVING

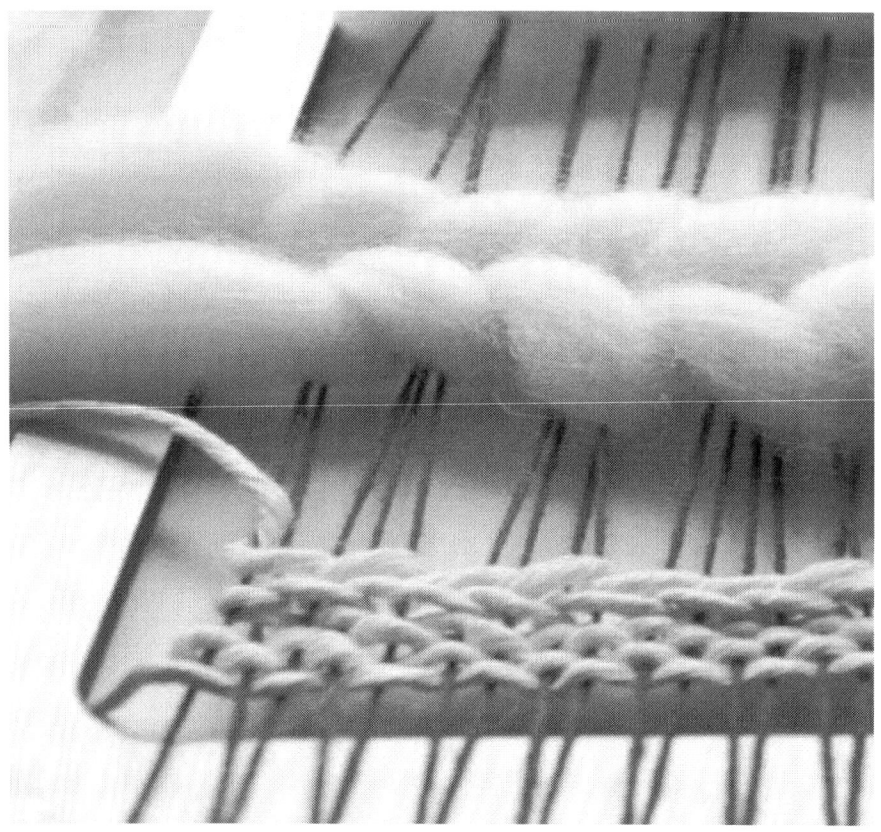

I wrote earlier that different ways of using pile weaving are needed to create braids with a very different look. I had so much fun looking at different ways I use the technique that I also wanted to share a few different ways I found weaving soybeans for different weaves to look at.

BASIC STEPS

First step:

Thread the weft thread on the three warp threads on the left side of the loom

Step 2:

For the third warp, move your weft thread under and around the third warp so that your weft thread is back on the chain.

Step 3:

Run your weft on the third, fourth, and fifth chains, then loosen it under and around the fifth chain.

Step 4:

Repeat this pattern to go through three chains and turn around the third until you reach the end.

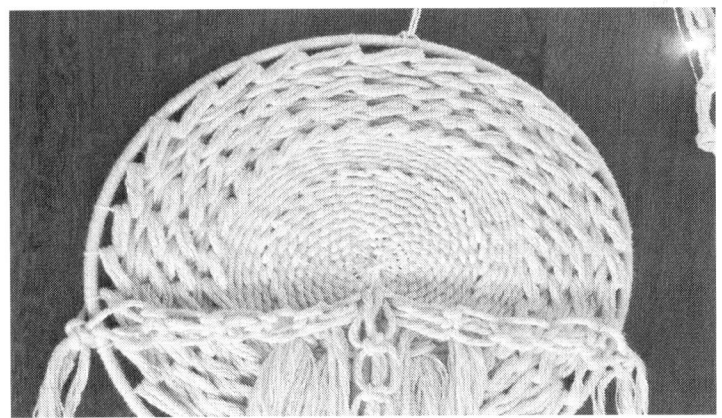

Soumak woven basket

I think what created this work was that woven circular texture. But it probably also helped that I used two strands of cotton ribbon that gave me a weaving-like texture like a basket. I wove a series of sauces, then a simple texture, then the same pulling pattern, and repeated. He made an interesting basket texture, which became larger as the string moved to the outside of the ring.

Soumak random lines

For some of my braids, I placed one row of sponge at an angle and then filled the gap with a smooth texture. This results in a really interesting and delicate design in the texture and compared to the large rows of textures, it catches the eye.

Qasab Soumak

The favorite of all time textures! Then weave the two rows of sponge textures and attach the "sponge" sponge to make them look like textures.

Woven chain

When I used one bulky (not super bulky) thread and threw it over a few warp threads so as not to completely cover the space, it looked like a woven chain. This is done in the same way as a woven fabric, with the difference that I intentionally leave space around the two rows soak to see the shape of the chain properl

Fishtail Soumak

I like how this technique looks. In the first row, he uses the usual slow soumak technique, and then in the second row, he distributes the soaking so that his bumps bend between the bumps of the first row. This creates what looks like a wolf texture.

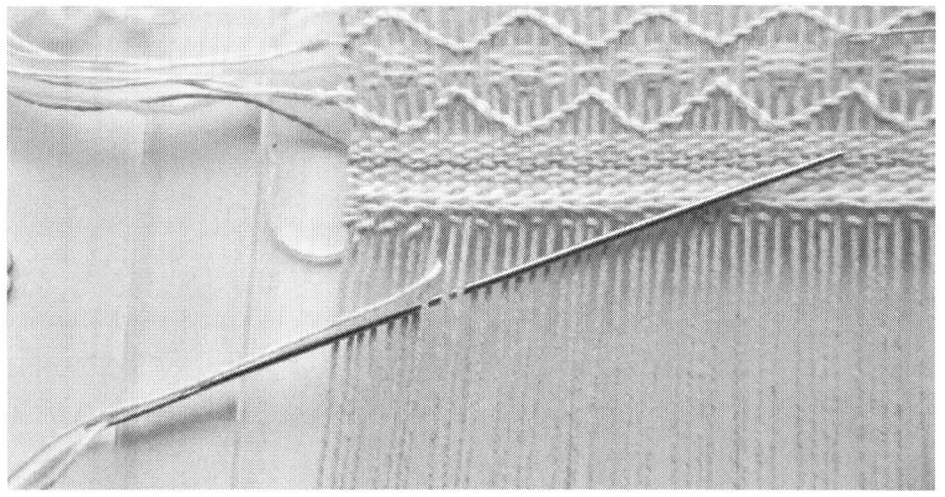

Reverse Soumak

This is a very fun way to use soy weaving differently. The technique is the same, except that the wetting is done on the back of the texture. This will show the loops around the warp thread at the beginning of the weave, then there will be small dotted weft threads. While weaving, I made two rows of inverted sponges that made a cute pattern from the dots.

Layered Rows of Soumak

When soaking and packing several rows of sauces, make interesting rolls. This works well especially when the soumak are woven by weaving at a fluffy angle.

How did you use the sponge in your braids? Have you tried anything new with it, or is there a certain way to use the soak you are taking advantage of? I like the cords, but I like to play with the technique and see what else can be done.

PILE WEAVE LOOPS

This pattern requires one or two bars or a thin, circular shape around which the wall can be wrapped.

Before you begin, weave a few rows or a simple weave to create a base for the pattern.

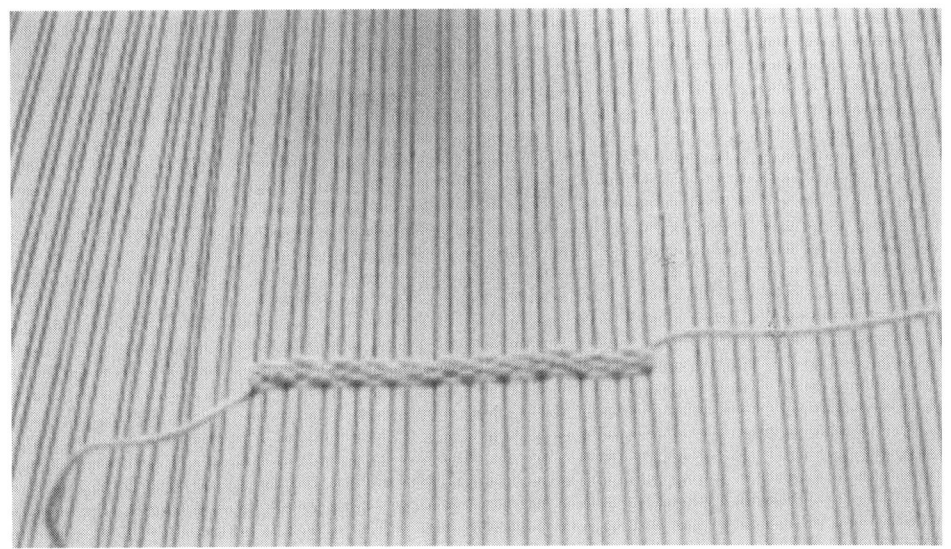

1. Loosely weaving is a series of smooth weaving.

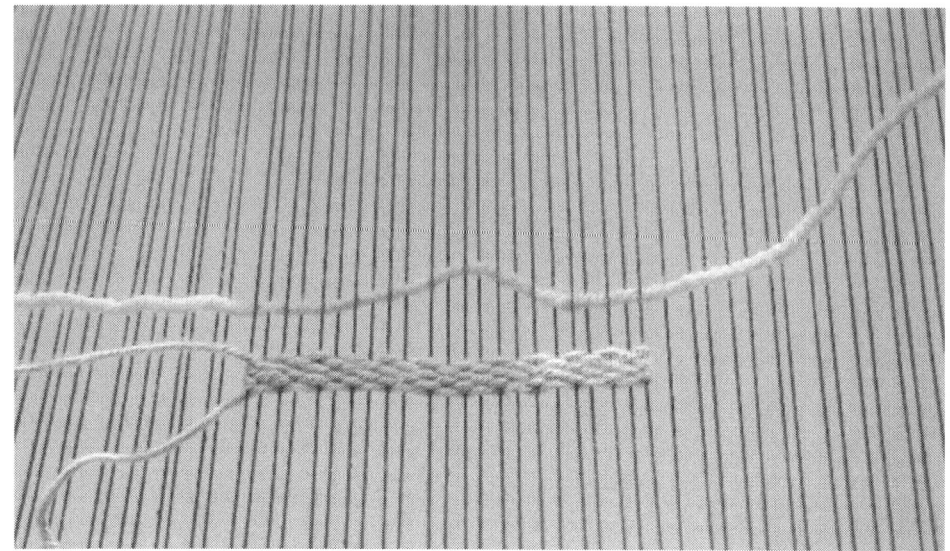

2. Carefully place the rod between the first part of the chain.

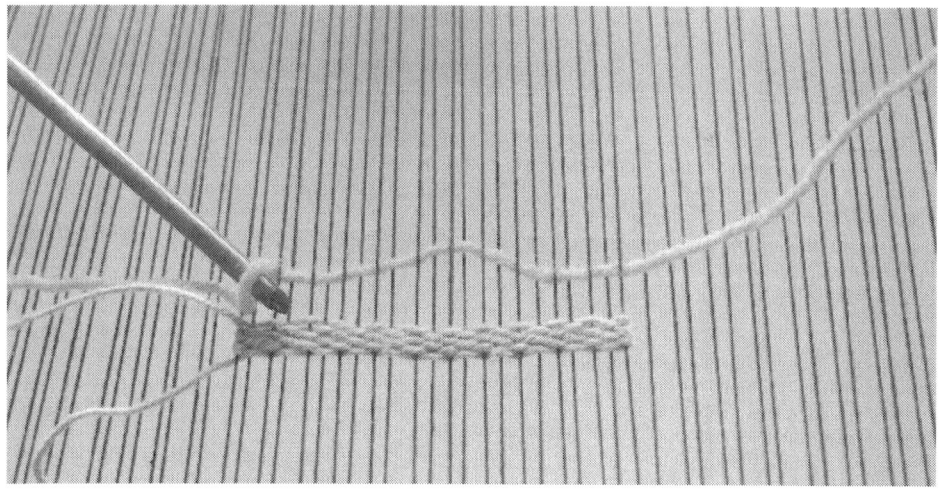

Don't be discouraged if the first time it doesn't work so easily. If necessary, use your fingers to help guide the wall around the bar.

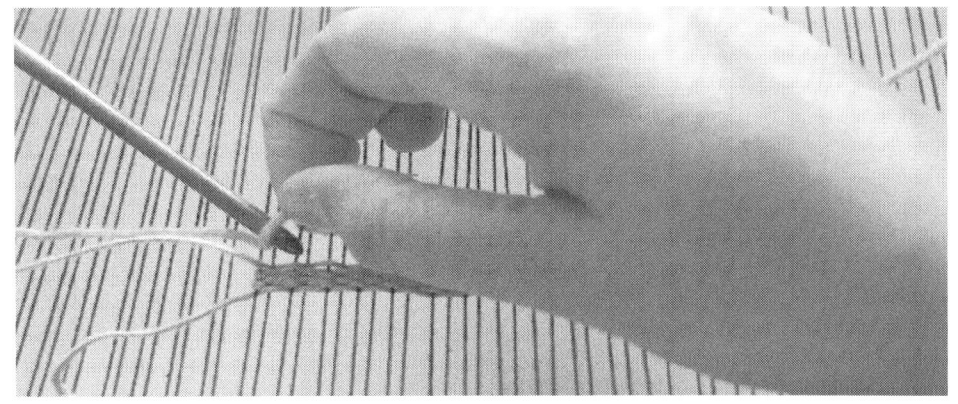

3. Rotate the wall with the bar in a rotating motion.

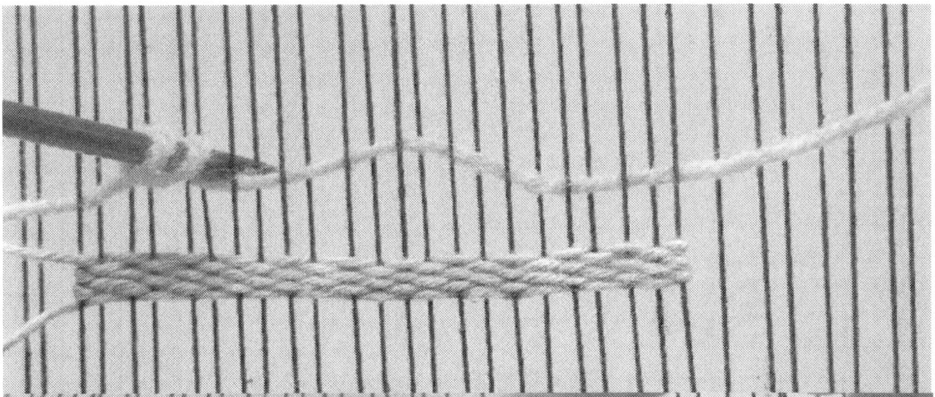

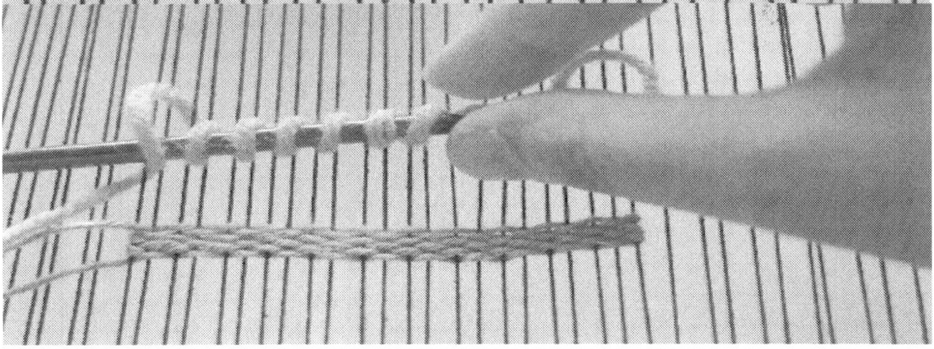

4. Continue this until the last warp thread. Hold the rod in place.

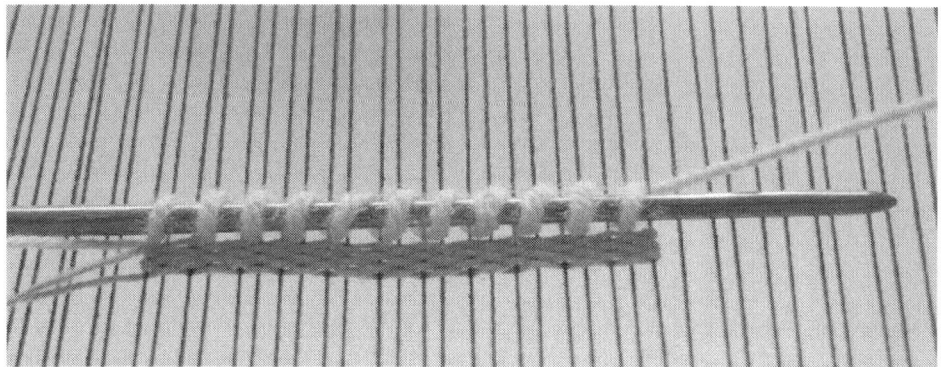

5. Weave a series of smooth braids and fasten the lines in place.

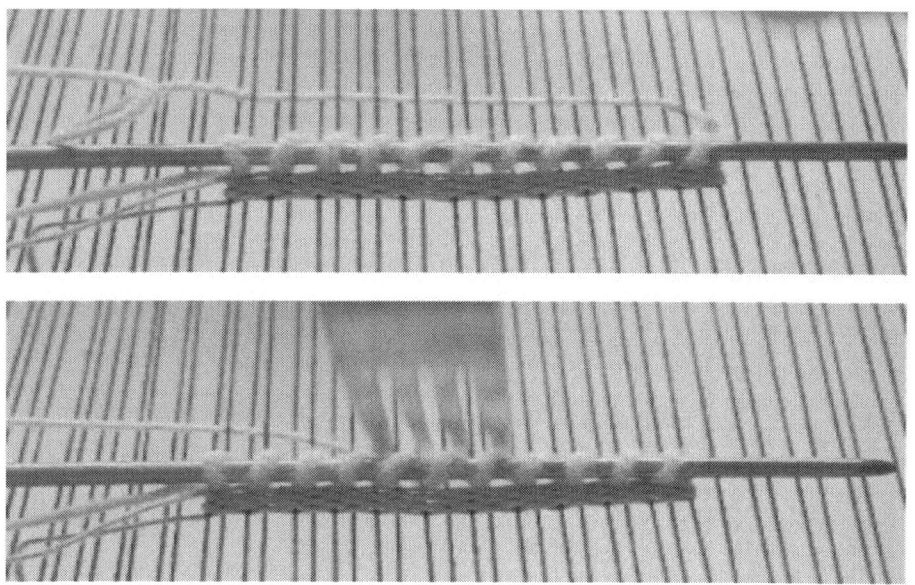

It was removed under the rod. However, if you want to build a few rows of fur textures, hold the rod in place.

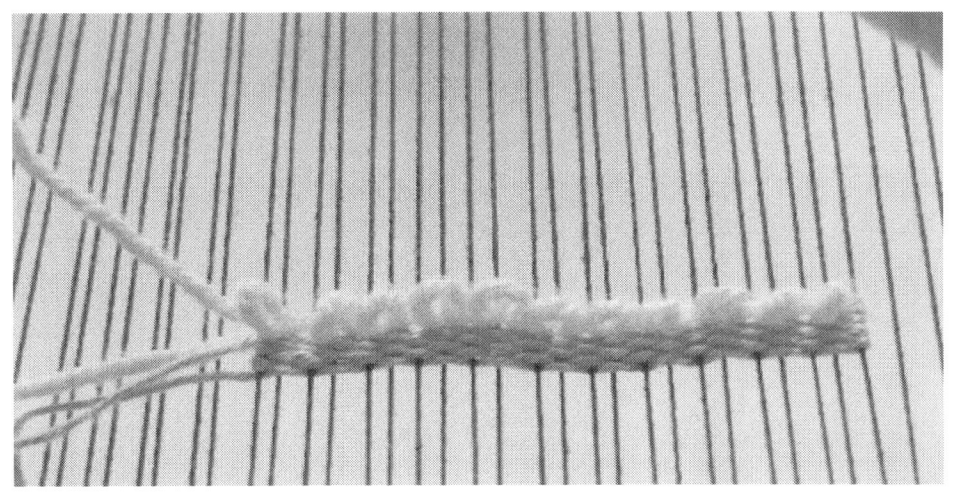

Prepare the model with several rows of piles. In the following pictures, note the pattern at the top.

6. Use the second bar to connect the threads in the second row (follow the same instructions as # 2- # 4).

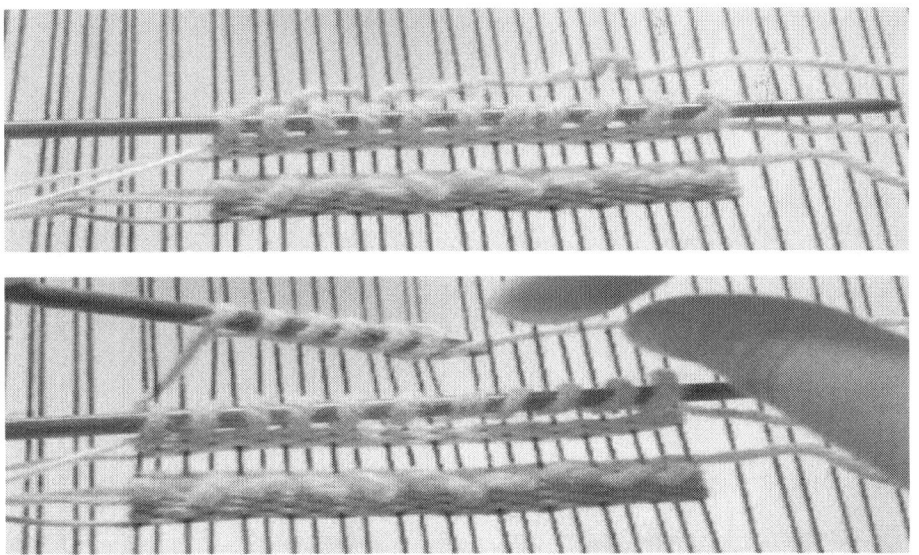

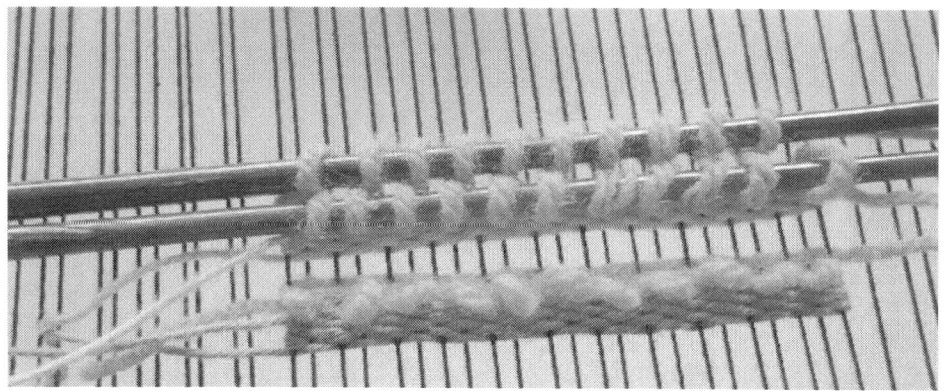

To secure the lines, 2-3 rows of plain weave should be woven behind each stack.

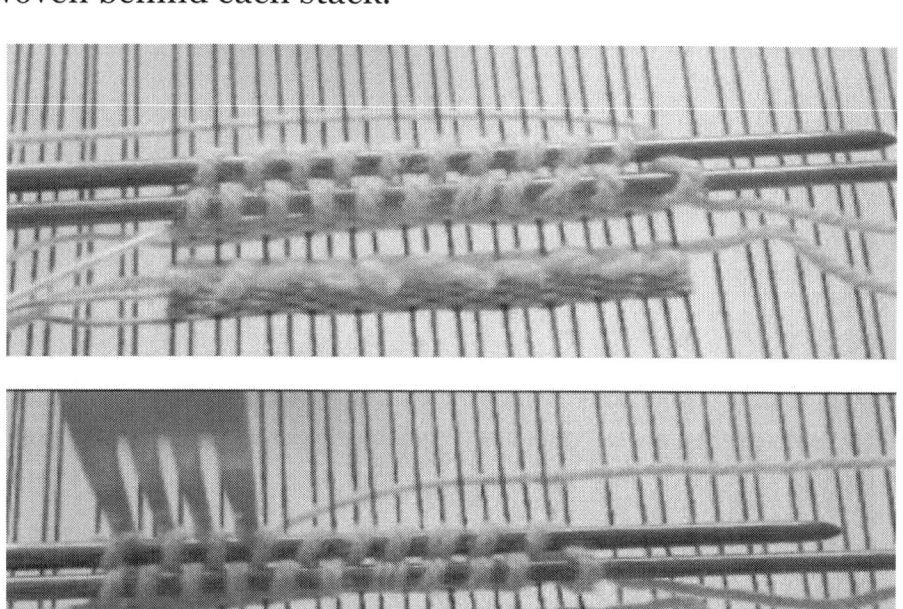

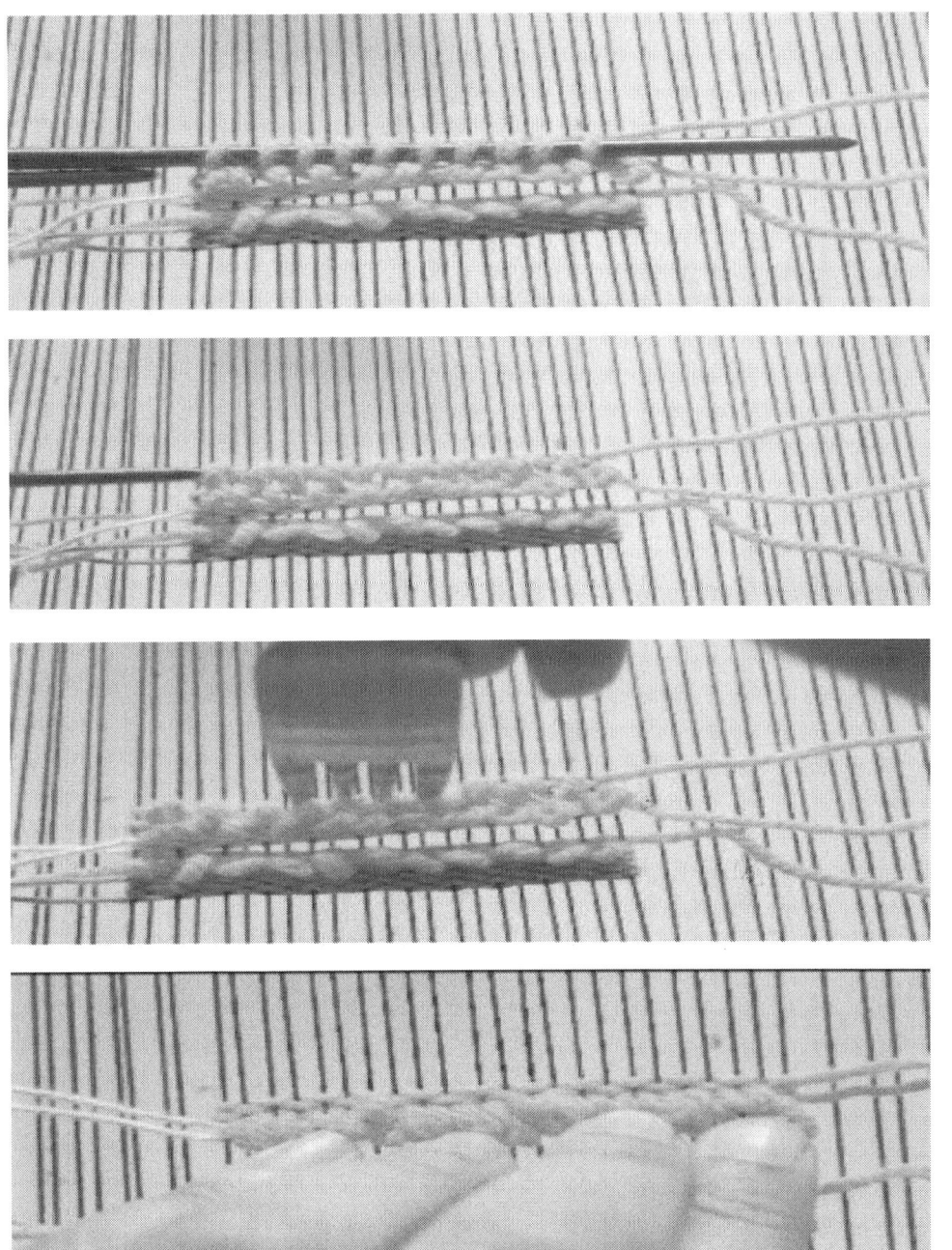

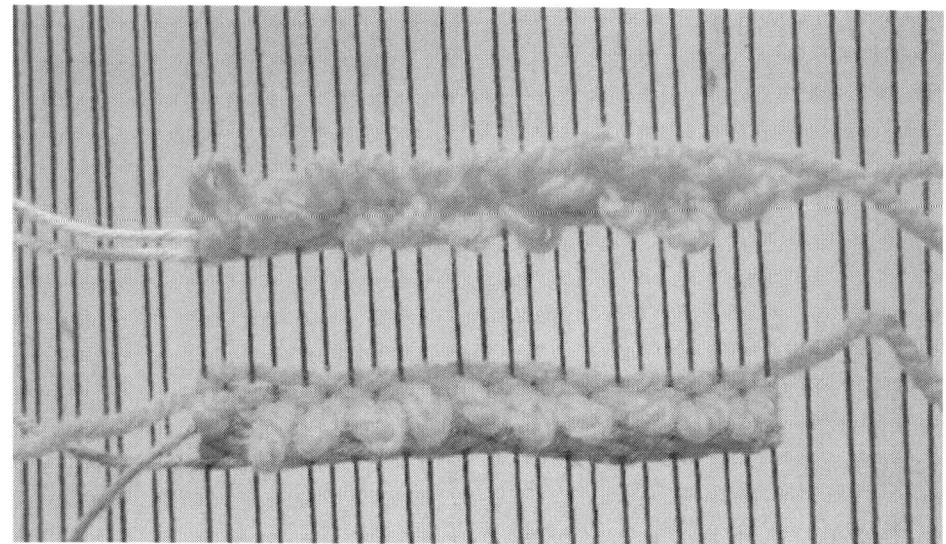

TIP: You can experiment with texture by lengthening the lines or adding a piece of fur texture to your piece.

Conclusion

Trends are just part of the weaving of the plan. You will find that the yarns of different textures and layers look different and affect the appearance of the pattern. Weaving opens up many possibilities for designing fiber art in different ways.

CHAPTER SEVEN

FINISH YOUR WOVEN PIECE

Congratulations on finishing weaving! It's time to end it. Depending on which loom (plain frame or cut frame) you used to create the texture, this affects the completion of the texture.

I did a texture finishing test with a stapler that provides a cleaner surface (in my opinion). So look at the two tuning techniques and choose which one works best.

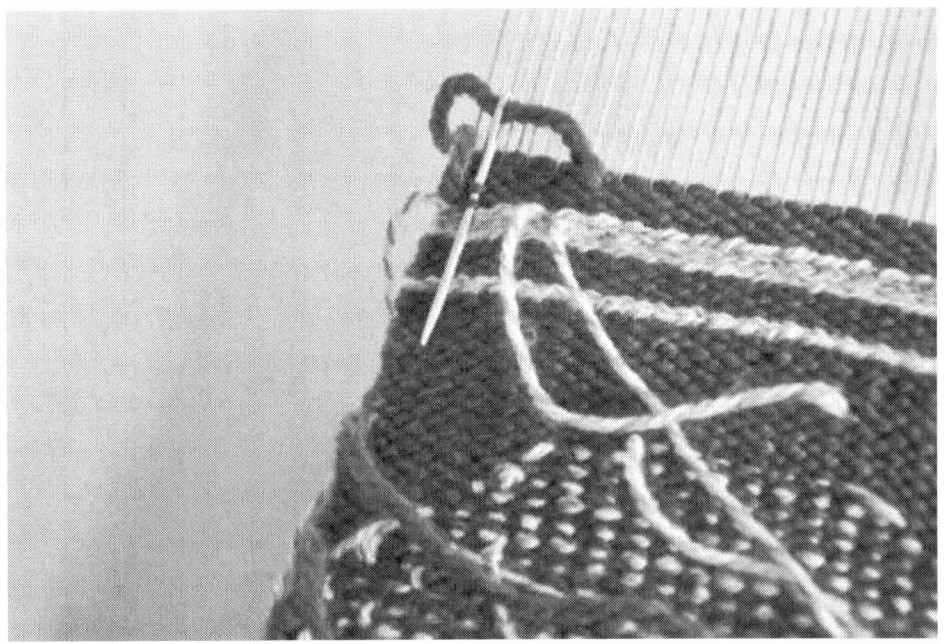

Finish weave 1

Start by taking a tapestry needle and weave the loose threads on the back of the weave. If you have yarns of different colors in your texture, be sure to weave the loose colors into the woven area of the same color to make sure the colors don't appear at the beginning of the texture. I also make sure to rotate my texture in the meantime to make sure I didn't cause any problems at the beginning of my texture. Pulling the wall tightly from the back, for example, can result in unsightly swelling in the front.

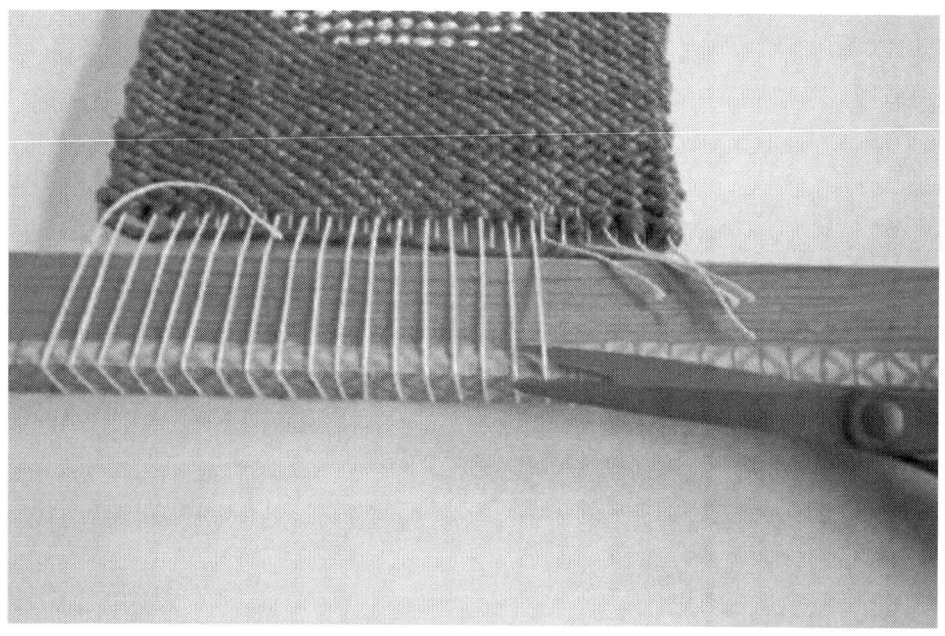

Finish weave 2

To finish with a simple frame fabric, cut the warp threads from the top of the frame, tie the two warp threads together, and then weave the back edge of the warp. If you don't want to finish weaving by tying the ends of the chain, read my post when you finish sewing.

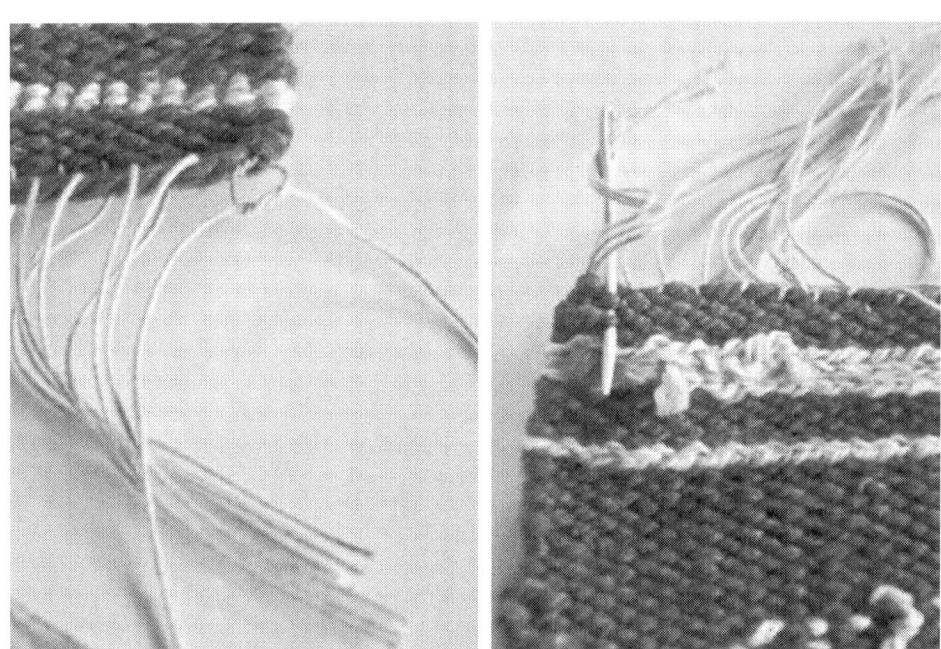

Finish weave 3

After you have finished the upper warp, do the same with the lower warp.

Then cut the long tail of the warp yarns pulled from behind the weave.

Finish weave 4

Now take a few yarns or warp yarns and attach them tightly to the warp yarns in your weave, wrap it around the rod or stick from which you will gather your weave.

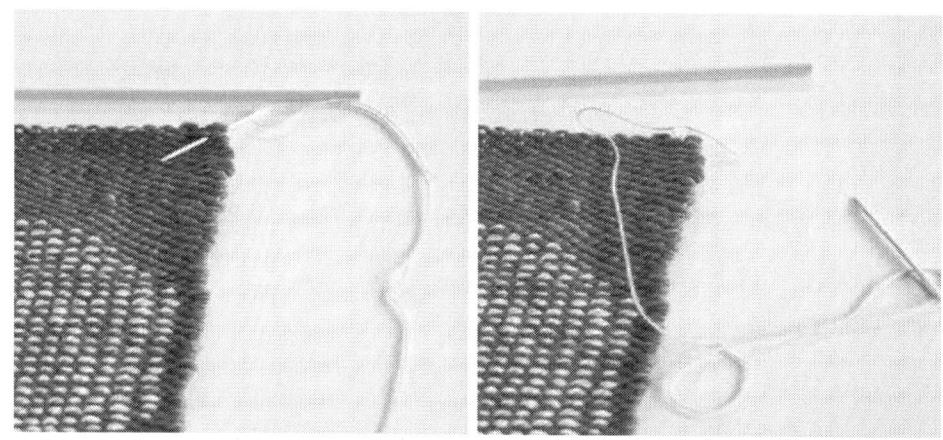

Finish weave 5

Pull back the warp thread at the top of the fabric into the warp thread, with about three spaces. Continue this method until you reach the end of the weave and tie a secure double knot with the warp thread.

Finish weave 6

Purchase another length of warp thread that is long enough to hang your texture now that it is attached to a hanging rod or coil. A good estimate of the length would be about twice the width of the texture. Be sure to connect this warp thread to both ends of the stick or stick.

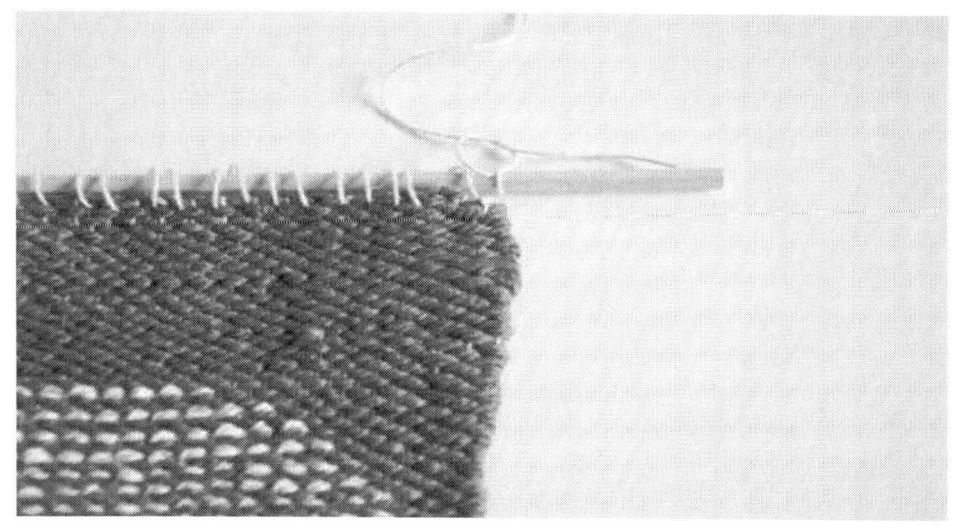

Finish weaving 7

To finish on the string, remove the upper chain links from the front pins/notches and place the metal pin or rod on which the fabric hangs. You can also use a natural strand to set up your texture if you wish, as long as the fabric you are using is a few inches wider than your texture. For the lower warp lines, follow the same steps as for the simply framed loom (above).

MAKE YOUR LOOM

You can use the cardboard loom as many times as you want, but eventually, it starts to break.

1. To make your cardboard, use the cardboard from a box instead of throwing it away and making it any size.

2. Measure ½ inch lines and mark at the top and bottom of the loom.

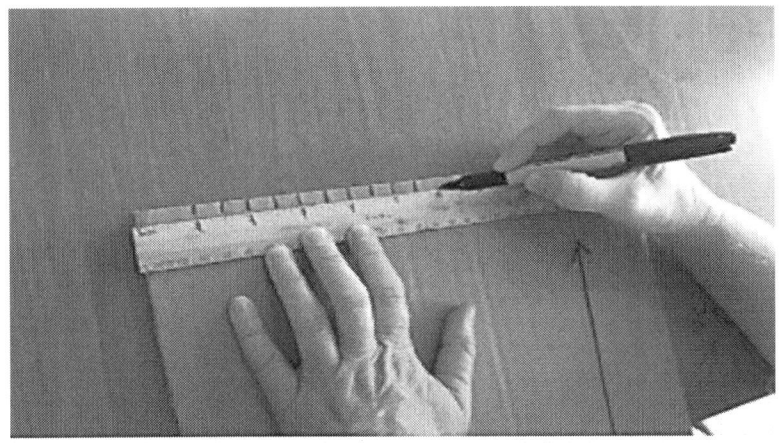

Measuring 1/2 inch lines

Mark the top and bottom of your loom.

3. Cut those "ears" with scissors on both the top and bottom

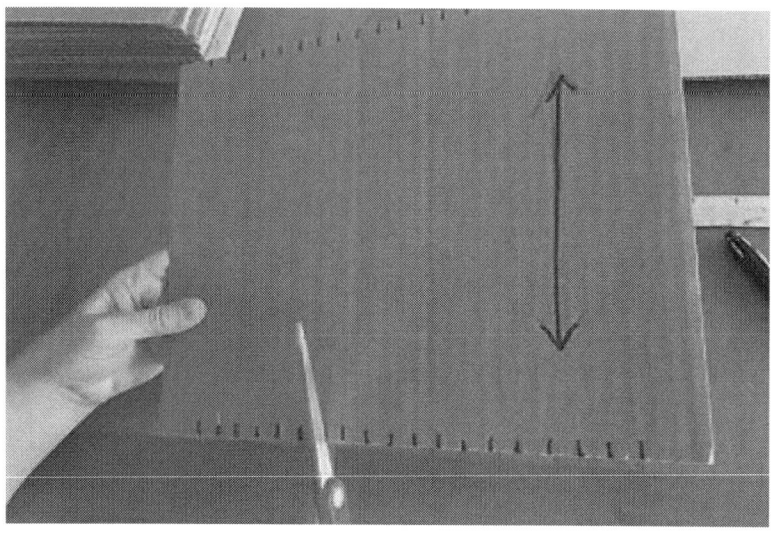

Cut the "ears" with scissors.

4. Place the warp threads by first sticking to the back of the loom and then running it through the front slot of the tabs.

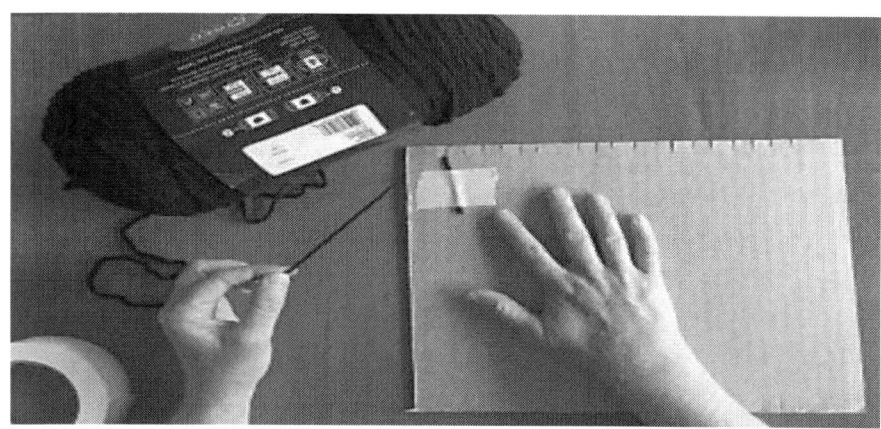

Apply the warp thread by sticking it on the back of the loom first

Move the thread forward through the front opening of the tabs.

5. Hold the warp tension, pass it through the slots and on the back of each tab, from top to bottom and back, until the warp thread is on the loom.

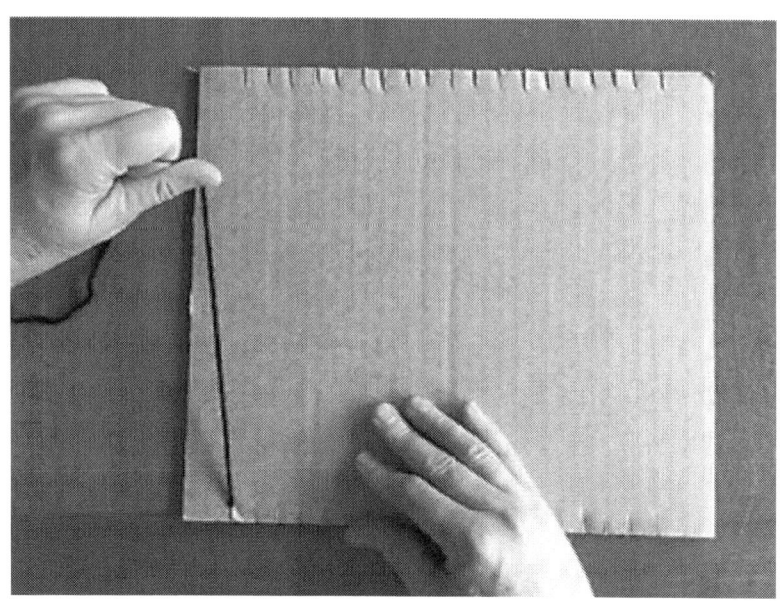

Pass the warp thread through the slots while holding it tight.

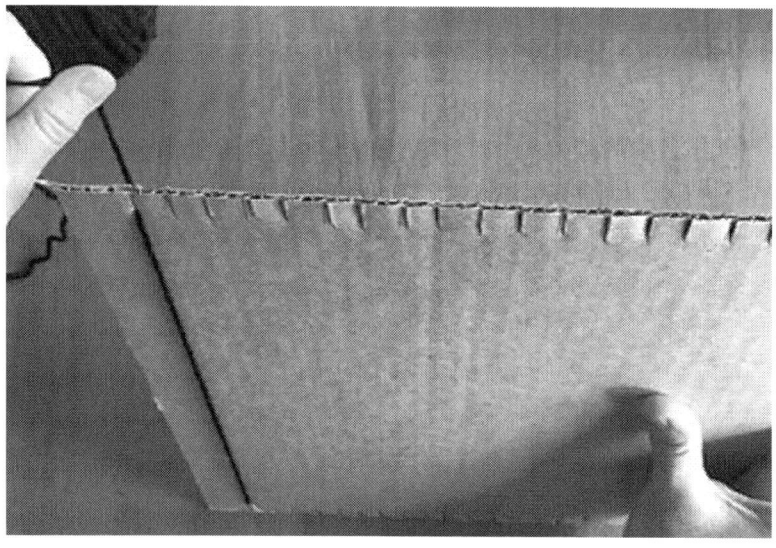

Running the yarn through the slots

Threading the loom

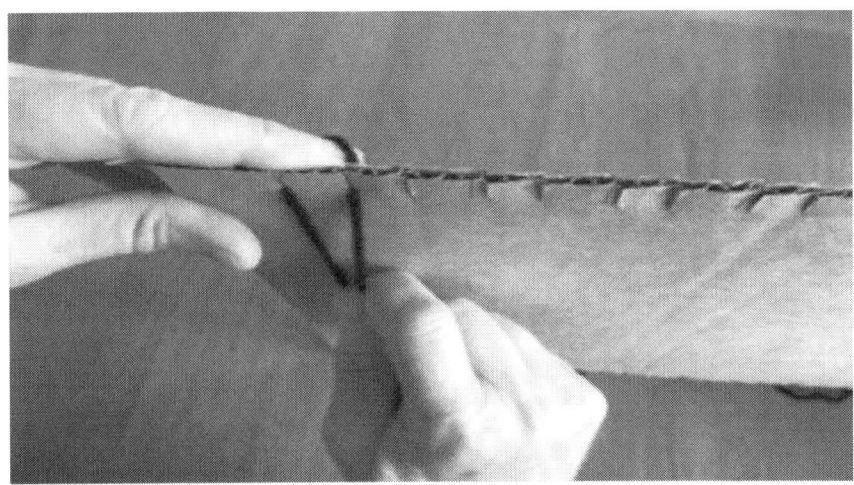

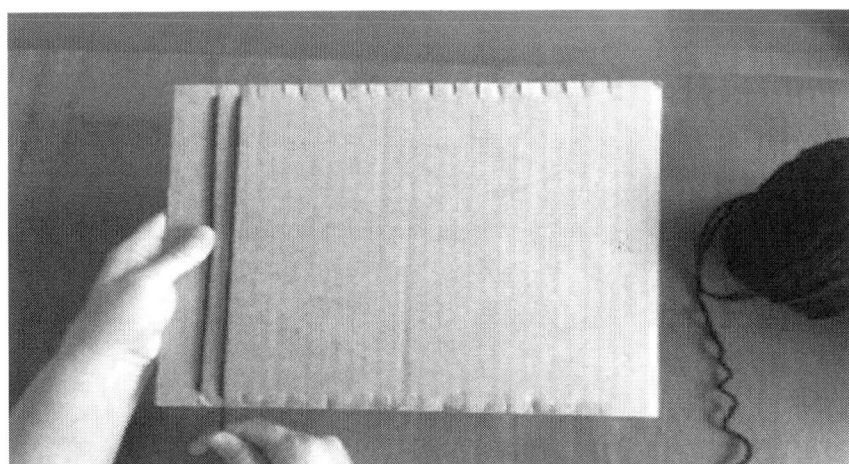

It stretches from the top of the wall to the bottom.

6. Glue the other end of the warp to the back of the loom when it is finished.

BRANCH WEAVING

Accessories:

- "T" shaped branch
- Gold tempera paint (I used this, which I found at my local art store, but it's cheaper on Amazon, just a little yellow)
- Yarn (you chose about 8 colors, but you can do whatever you want!)
- Plastic needles
- Pony beads (optional - used beads)
- Pom-pom maker - the smallest size (or just use your favorite technique)
- Good scissors
- Mask tape

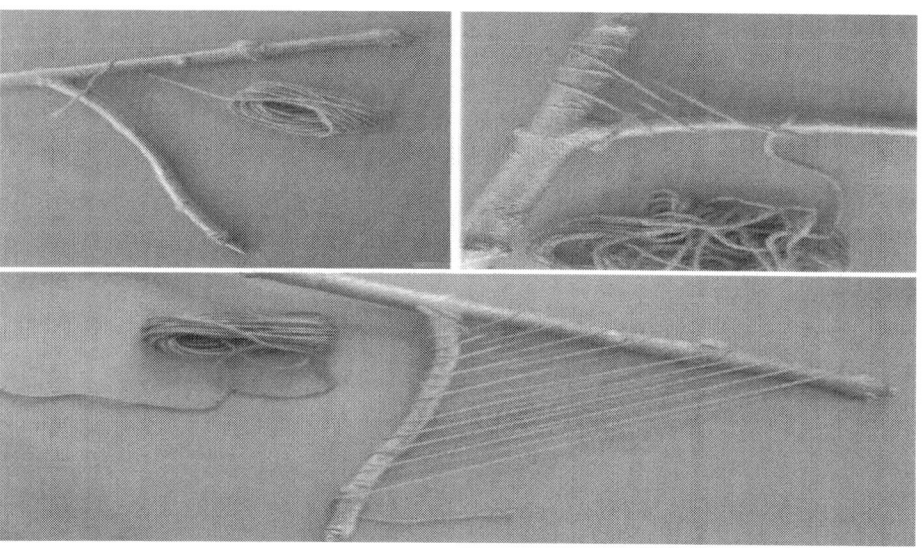

Make a lovely weaving out of a common branch.

PROCESS:

- Paint your arm first.
- Then turn the wall around to create the warped wall. Shake it and then tie it to fix it. It was still a bit lose and weak, but it fell into place as I started to make the weft (this thread connecting the chain).

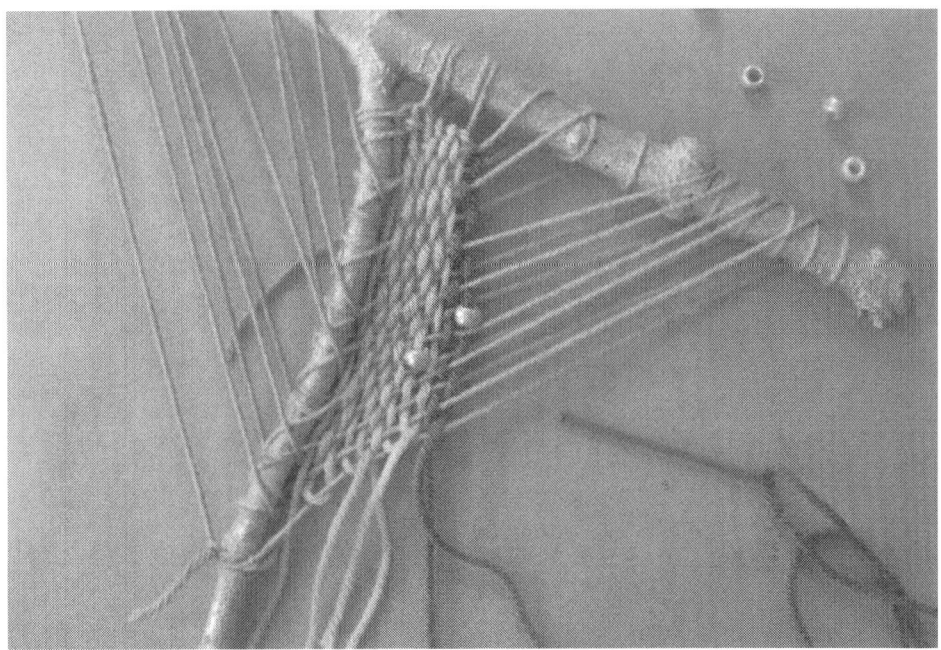

- Then start weaving. Above and below. If you want to change the color, just cut at the bottom and start again. I forgot some beads on one side. I thought maybe I should play with the asymmetry of the stick.

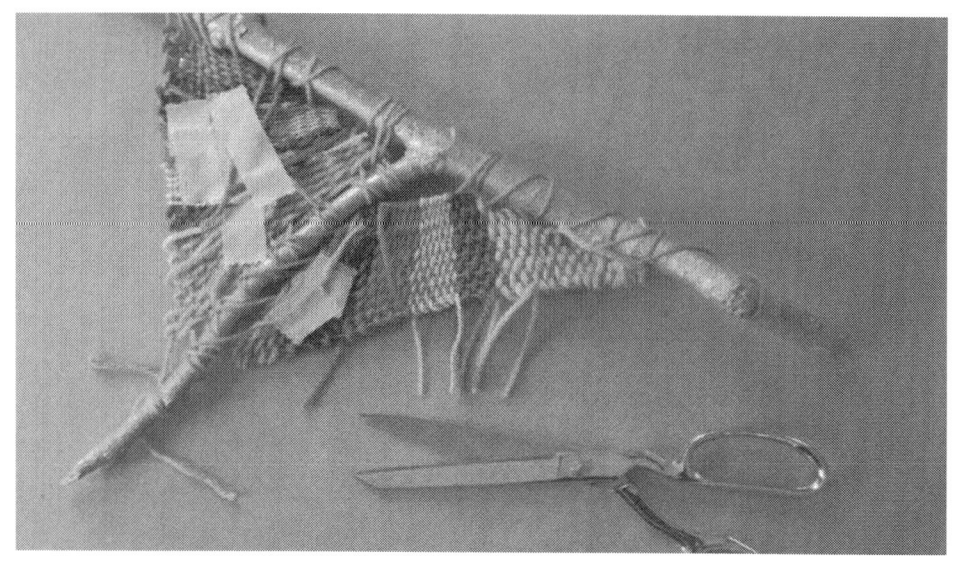

➢ Loosen the loose threads as you go on the back. They are annoying when hanging anywhere.

- Make pom-poms. I did half a thing with me. Be sure to leave a tail.
- Put them on the branch to figure out the order. Now tie them to the top and cut off the sin.

- I wrapped yarn around the dot at the bottom and knotted knots on the back.

SUMMER BRACELET

Easy bracelets are good crafts that you can take anywhere! They are especially nice for those who have failed to learn to work and crochet. As a bonus, I feel that learning an easy bracelet is one of those rites of passage you always do at summer camp, so maybe it's just like figuring out how to ride a bike again.

All you need to make a friendship bracelet is a little silk embroidery! In this guide, I'll show you how to make the most basic bracelets - the candy bar!

You may make them as thick or thin as you choose, and learning how to make a simple bracelet in less than an hour is much easier. You will move faster and faster too!

FIRST STEP:

What you need:

> - Silk embroidery / thin yarn
> - Scissors
> - Tape or pins/ safety pins

Embroidery silk can be cheap in such huge packages! You don't have to be fashionable. Make sure you have six strands - otherwise it won't be thick enough for a beautiful brooch.

Lion Brand yarns also have these little thread buttons called perfect Bonbons. And, they are cute.

The ribbon or pins hold the bracelet in place while turning/connecting the bracelet easily.

STEP 2:

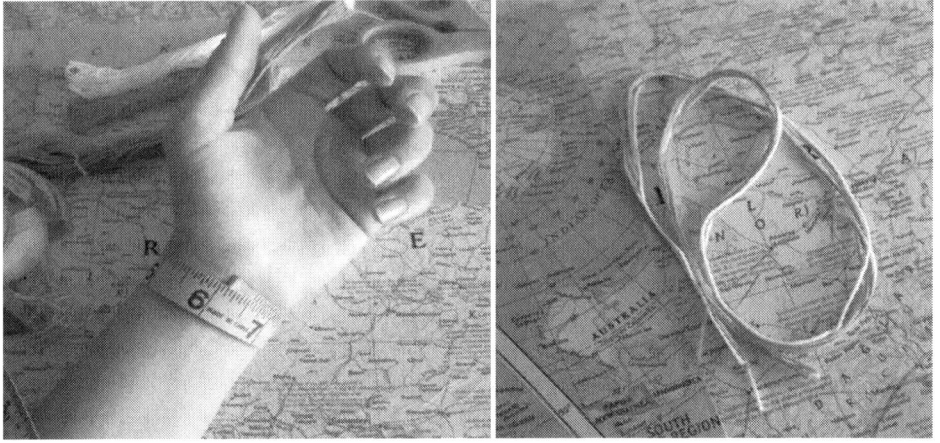

Measurement + cutting

As a general rule, cut pieces of dental floss the length between your fingertips and shoulders - I can say that a nail of about 30 inches works well for me! I tried the 25 with the first one and it cut me very close.

My wrist is approx. It's about 6 inches, so let's say you measure your wrist and then multiply that by 5 to be safe. You don't want to end up without a dental floss behind the knot and you can't finish.

If you are going to make a bracelet of more than six lines, you may want to add another 6 inches! You make extra knots for each row, so it goes through each color a little faster.

STEP 3:

DETERMINATION OF THE NUMBER OF YARNS

Most yarns I've ever made are eight. I usually go six - six is perfect for me - fine but detailed, and finally approx. 1 / 4-1 / 3 inches.

Keep in mind that a larger number of cords is harder to keep track of, and the brooch may bend slightly due to more cords, so you need to block it (see the last step on how to do this!) If you want it to lie down right.

And depending on what you want in your pattern, you can use two alternating colors, or each thread can be a different color. You can get very small samples with little effort!

STEP 4:

Start the bracelet by taking the cut strips of the embroidered dental floss and tying together an excess knot at one end.

Glue this on the tabletop or pants or pillows and weave three inches under this knot. After you have finished your weave, make another knot at the bottom of the weave.

And now we come to the fun part!

To be clear, each final bracelet contains 3 inches of braid on both ends (for a total of 6 inches) and 3-4 inches of real bracelet that forms the knot.

STEP 5:

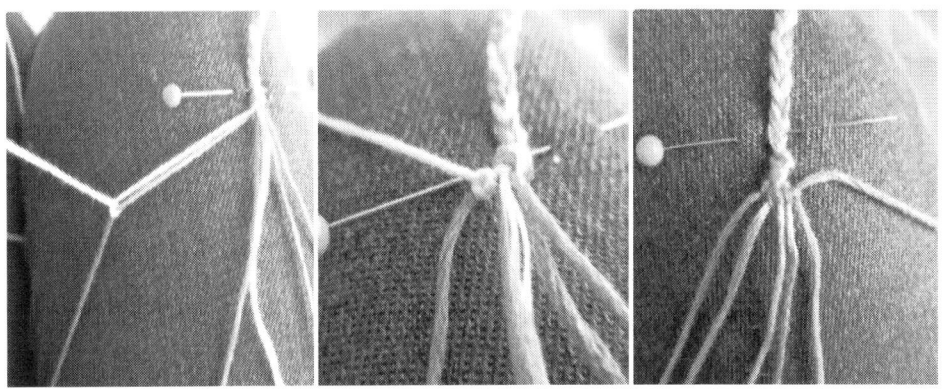

Start the Knotting

To make the grooved surface, which looks woven of an easy bracelet, you need to make a lot of small knots.

You must first decide in what order the yarns should be. This determines the color order of the rows.

If they are good, pick up the first two threads. The farthest wall to the left creates the first row. To achieve this, knot around the other lines of dental floss/yarn.

1. Remove the first thread and transfer it to the second thread, then to the back as shown. It is important to connect the second thread, this will give it a proper appearance.
2. Now hold the second thread tightly and pull the first thread up and toward the large knot. Pull until you find resistance, but no harder! This creates a small knot on the second thread.

3. Make another knot by tying the first thread around the second thread again - just repeat what you did before.
4. Continue in the right direction, use the first thread to create two knots for each bracelet thread.
5. After connecting to the right and reaching the last thread/thread, start the first thread on the left again. Be sure to make two knots on each thread.
6. Continue until knots 3-4 centimeters.

STEP 6:

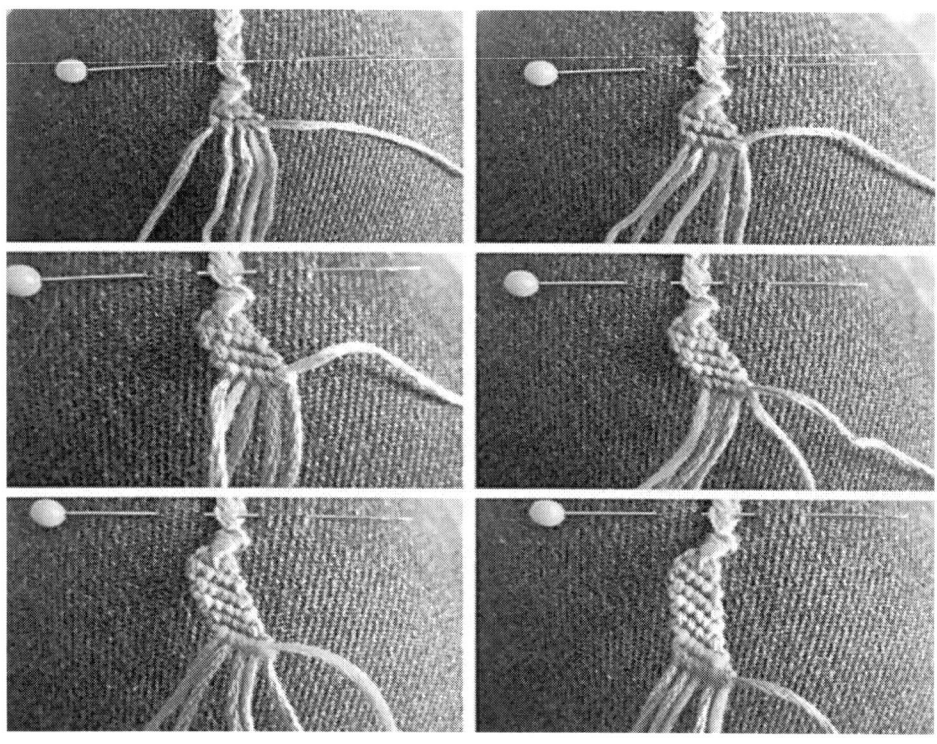

As will be seen during the trip

I feel it's a useful way to understand what you're doing.

As you can see, it only works with color on the left and makes two knots on the right. The color you just made on the right hangs to the side all the time, making it easier to finish the line.

If a wall is missing or you accidentally forget to complete the line, it should be noticeable easily. It's a good idea to hold a needle to make it easier to grip the knots if shaking - they're so tiny it's hard to make them with your fingers!

STEP 7:

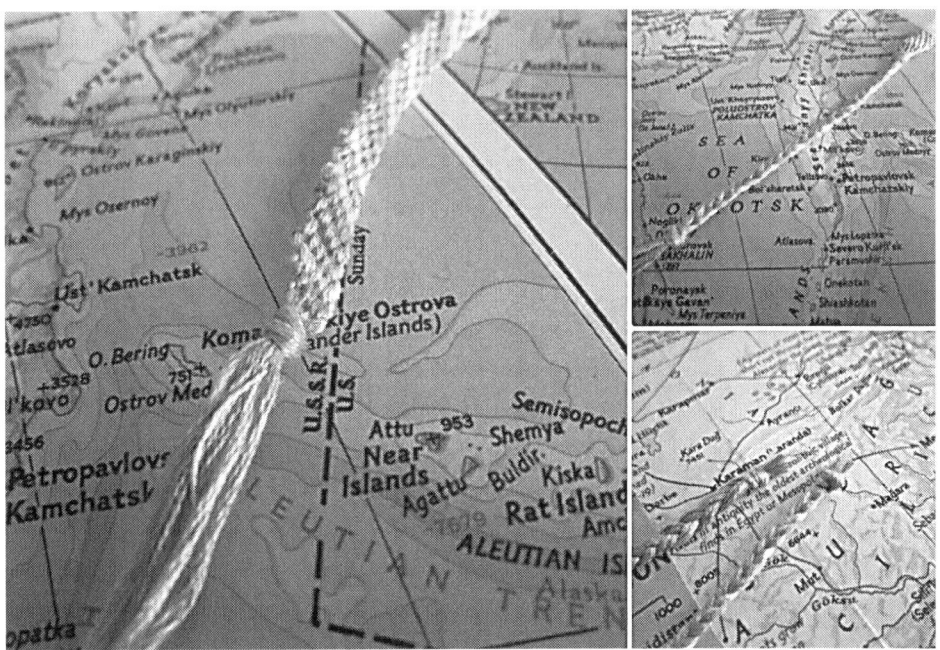

How to Finish the Bracelet

After connecting 3-4 inches, the bracelet will work well.

Make another knot at the end of the main part of the bracelet. Weave three inches of that knot and then knot again.

Now cut the extra dental floss/thread from both ends of the bracelet. This is done now!

STEP 8:

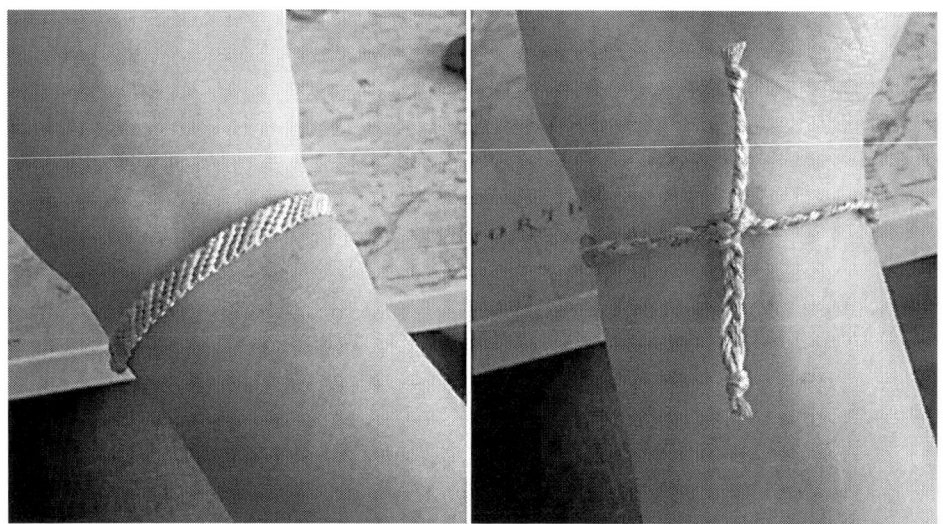

Tie It On

With weaving, as we did, it would be very easy to tie/untie. And you can do it yourself.

They no longer have to take a shower and walk around with wet bracelets for hours! (I swear it always happened when I was making them when I was younger, or when my friend made one for me and tied it up. I wasn't allowed to remove them. It was either worn or cut and ruined: P)

STEP 9:

If you wrap your bracelet in anger, it will bend slightly. To overcome this, you can stick it to a flat surface. Check to see if it's nice and tight.

Spray a good amount of water on it (soak it!) And let it dry. This is called "blocking" and helps it lie firmly and flat.